THE
HEIGHTS
OF THE HILLS
ARE HIS ALSO

THE
HEIGHTS
OF THE HILLS
ARE HIS ALSO

CHRISTOPHER R. SEITZ

BAYLOR UNIVERSITY PRESS

Cover and book design by Elyxandra Encarnación
Cover art: William Blake (1757–1827), *The Vision of Christ*. Illustration of the Book of Job. Watercolor. RA 2001.79. The Morgan Library & Museum, New York, NY / Art Resource, NY.

Library of Congress Cataloging-in-Publication Data

Names: Seitz, Christopher R., author.
Title: The heights of the hills are His also / Christopher R. Seitz.
Description: Waco, Texas : Baylor University Press, [2024] | Summary: "Engages with a selection of Psalms and the book of Job to draw attention to the inner logic of Scripture's witness, combining elements of the personal and spiritual, theological and critical"— Provided by publisher.
Identifiers: LCCN 2024025213 (print) | LCCN 2024025214 (ebook) | ISBN 9781481322454 (hardcover) | ISBN 9781481322485 (adobe pdf) | ISBN 9781481322478 (epub)
Subjects: LCSH: Bible. Psalms—Criticism, interpretation, etc. | Bible. Job—Criticism, interpretation, etc. | Creation—Biblical teaching.
Classification: LCC BS1430.52 .S445 2024 (print) | LCC BS1430.52 (ebook) | DDC 223/.206—dc23/eng/20240814
LC record available at https://lccn.loc.gov/2024025213
LC ebook record available at https://lccn.loc.gov/2024025214

Contents

Preface   vii
Acknowledgments   xiii

Introduction   1

PART I   THE PSALMS OF CREATION

The Psalms and the Majesty of God the Creator   11

Psalm 29   15

Psalms 46 and 69   19

Psalms 93 and 96   23

The Tides of the Psalter   27

Book Four of the Psalter   35

The Majesty of God in Creation   41

Ascent and Alleluia   45

PART II   THE WITNESS OF JOB

The Majesty of the Creator and His World   55

The Freedom of Job and of God   59

God Answers Job   65
Tone and Form

The Majesty of Creation in Job and in the Psalms   71

The Divine Response   75

Zoological Wonder   81

Job, Behemoth, and Leviathan   85
God's Final Address

Response and Restoration   91

Job Alive Again   95
The Book's Finale

Conclusion   97

For Further Study   101

Preface

The present book pays attention to the character of two large-scale compositions in the Scriptures of Israel, typically grouped side by side in canonical lists, the Psalms and the book of Job. By "character" I refer to the cumulative effect achieved by the compositional history of these works, now given to us in the final form, or canonical shape, in which they come to us.

This compositional history has been the source of detailed examination since the nineteenth century, with the intent to "place in order" the history of the coming-to-be of both works. One can see in these studies various degrees of persuasiveness, and it is doubtless the case that the final form of the Psalter and of Job is the result of a rich diachronic history. To speak of the character of the Psalter or Job, as I will mean it here, is to put that history, and the theories about it, in service to our appreciation of the achievement represented by the final form. The final form of both works represents a rich and sophisticated amalgamation whose heritage has been directed to just this achievement and just this appreciation.

At points along the way, the findings of historical-critical work will be referenced, but only with an eye to understanding the achievement represented by, respectively, the five-book form of the Psalter, or the way in which the Prologue, Dialogues, Elihu Speeches, Divine Response, and Epilogue (the typically declared constituent parts of the book of Job) have been so ordered and coordinated to speak forth the message of this outstanding biblical witness.

The theological category we pursue in both contexts is God in creation. This is an obvious theme in the Psalter. What interests us is the way in which it has been developed across the final form of the 150-psalm collection.

For the book of Job, an examination of God in creation in the Psalms forms an indispensable step in appreciating how God has chosen to speak to his exemplary protagonist, the stricken man Job, in the Divine Speeches represented by chapters 38–41.

The (more recently developed) model for reading the book of Job has focused on questions of authorial location, the development of the ingredient parts it contains, and how Job might be interpreted vis-à-vis a category called wisdom literature. This latter category is now under careful scrutiny and reevaluation.

For our present purpose, however, what recourse to such a classification tended to do was speak of increasing degrees of skepticism, with Proverbs on the front end and Ecclesiastes at the end point. Job fell in the middle. And in the middle, it charted its own similar journey from piety to despair (or simple resignation before the mystery of suffering, or a God that empirical "wisdom" was unable to disclose or even speak meaningfully about). Job's initial piety and forbearance collapsed under the weight of the suffering he had to endure, God's response was unintelligible or even hostile, Elihu appeared to mitigate that (somehow), and the book ended in a brief and rather cliché fashion.

The obvious point of contact between Job and the Psalms (a work not included in the usual wisdom classification) was severed due to this way of approaching Job. Within the wisdom category itself, the most obvious link has always been between Proverbs and Ecclesiastes, and with them both, the Song of Songs—all with a form of attribution or association with the figure of Solomon. Job's inclusion disrupted or confused that obvious Solomonic association. Job—book and protagonist—are not all that obviously related to Proverbs and Ecclesiastes.

This has become all the more obvious due to the recent pressure to question the category "wisdom literature" itself and wonder about its ongoing utility and helpfulness for reading these individual witnesses and appreciating them as individual accomplishments. The Solomonic books are classified as such, in my view, not due to claims about authorship, but rather due to a canonical shaping encouraging us to read them as complementary witnesses. This includes, for example, understanding why the name Solomon is not mentioned in Ecclesiastes, even as his presence obviously hovers over the opening chapters.

By moving to Job through the lens of God in creation in the book of Psalms, we wish to recenter the dramatic divine speeches. Form criticism had always recognized that God's speeches to Job by means of creation belonged to the same kind of genre as what we see in the Psalter. But they are also distinctive, and in order to appreciate that distinctiveness we must begin with what the Psalter presents as a way to measure and appreciate that.

Another thing needs to be said at this point. In our examination of the shape of the Psalter, we shall see that the idea of a "covenant with creation," undergirding and preceding the covenants God establishes in the sacred history with his people, is critical to the way the Psalter unfolds across its five-book form. This becomes especially obvious in Book Four, following upon the harsh judgment found at the close of Psalm 89, that God has severed his special bond with David.

We firmly believe that in order properly to understand the book of Job, the man Job must be allowed to live in the context the author of the book has set him in. He is the contemporary of Noah (as Ezek 14 has it). To confuse this imagined and highly significant location in time of the book's protagonist with a theory about the book's author and social-historical setting—a move typical in the history-of-religion approaches to Job—where "Job" is what such a setting might mean distorts our ability to hear what God says to him under the conditions the book has set before us. God cannot speak to Job of a sacred history that the book understands to be nowhere yet on the horizon. Karl Barth is correct to emphasize that the book's hero is a non-Israelite. More than that, he is a pre-Israelite, in the sense that the world he inhabits precedes the election of Abraham and the history that ensues in the light of that pivotal event (Gen 11).

So, when God speaks, he does so from the context of Job's special place in time. He speaks by means of creation. In this sense, the book of Job and the Psalms come alongside each other in important ways. It is God's reign and his control over creation that form the solid bulwark against all foes, and this reign will find itself coming into clearest frame in the Psalter when the series of covenants God has made with his people in history appear to be in abeyance. Now, as well, we can begin to move toward something of a clearer understanding of the way God's speech to Job, far from shutting him up or changing the subject, gives rise to a level of comprehension greater than anything he has yet to know or understand—and that while still on the ash-heap of his mortal coil and severely diminished existence.

I speak of this before we begin to indicate why I am treating the Psalter and Job together in this book. I believe the story to be told will make that clear as the reader moves along, but it is also helpful to explain something of the logic I am pursuing at the outset. Furthermore, the book to follow will not engage in lengthy discussions with the usual historical-critical questions. I have written widely on these matters elsewhere. I speak on the terms I do here, at the start, to lay out the general background of this scholarly terrain. Why I deal with creation in the Psalter and in Job should be obvious enough on its own terms, but there is also a legacy of reading Job as a part of wisdom literature, and the Psalter as belonging to its own specific context, that has prevented one from following where they occupy the same territory of theological and exegetical concern. That has, to my mind, hampered our ability to hear Job properly and to follow the central place creation has in the shape and movement of the Psalter.

We have now given a general background of this area of recent scholarly approaches. The heart of this book prefers to move ahead with a different tempo and feel, and only nod occasionally to this kind of formal inquiry and scholarly debate. There will be no footnotes. At the end of the treatment, I will provide the usual information one finds in the area of "for further study." It is my intention to write a book with its own genre and pace. I think this is the best way to pursue the topic of interest—that is, the majesty of God in creation.

A final note on the translations used here.

Scripture citations come from the Revised Standard Version, or from the Canticles of the Book of Common Prayer. The Bible is a special book on its own terms, but also because of the life it has in the long history of interpretation in church and in synagogue. It lives and breathes in that life. If for this reason alone, one cannot properly speak of language as "antiquated" or "non-inclusive," because our own place in time is but the latest in a long and rich history of the Bible sounding forth its unique notes and cadences within the choir of attentive hearers.

"The Heights of the Hills Are His Also" is language that lives in my deepest memory and the wellsprings of my worship life, going back into a time even before scholars gathered to produce what was called a "revised standard version" of the Bible. That it has come to be further "revised" makes the point nicely that we all live in a specific place and time and the Bible is forever there before us. And after us.

As is the God of creation.

Acknowledgments

My sincere thanks go to the excellent team at Baylor University Press. This is not a usual book. Dave Nelson encouraged me from the beginning, having read what I sent him. He also helped with the William Blake selections. Baylor graphic designer Elyxandra Encarnación worked hard to get the cover and art right. Cade Jarrell and Jenny Hunt oversaw the editing with aplomb.

My late wife always asked me to write a book for a general audience. She had done doctoral work herself, but knew the preaching side of me and wanted me to write in that vein. This present book has arisen in large measure due to the life we shared together and the sensibilities she encouraged in me. I dedicate it to her memory, ma femme, Elizabeth New Seitz.

INTRODUCTION

I was born at the elevation of 3,500 feet in the mountains of western North Carolina. Now, a hugely popular destination. Then, a summer retreat for those escaping the heat in Florida and adjacent states.

I attended a private, all-boys boarding school near Asheville when I turned fourteen. The most distinctive feature of the school, alongside several contenders, was the work program. The school had a paid cook and some staff in the kitchen, and a single individual who ran what was called "the shop," a dispensary of spades, mattocks, rakes, lawnmowers, saws, yard equipment, paint, brushes, mops, hammers, and a few power tools (chainsaws and less lethal weaponry).

A particularly memorable item was a product called sweeping compound, a reddish, oil-based, granular confection that you used to sweep floors. In big, corrugated bins. I can still smell it. I've never seen it anywhere since. You got a piece of stiff cardboard and ladled the compound on it, and then you were off to your sweeping assignment. It helped you see where you were sweeping, and it left a fine oily residue. Wooden floors were the rule, with some minor exceptions. Done with the sweeping, you collected what was left after its labor and threw it away, spent after doing its job.

The point of this is that the boys did all the manual labor. That included working at "the farm" (a small dairy and crop production on the premises), laying bricks, driving trucks (without a license), and all the big and small jobs of maintenance and repair a school of 125 boys, all boarders—all good at wearing things out—required. The headmaster was himself an accomplished builder and mason. I can see him on his hands and knees, an omnipresent Camel cigarette dangling from his mouth, pushing the board you used when laying brick walkways, helping to evenly distribute the sand.

It was a great system, saved the school money, and taught boys how to work and be held responsible for it. Since we were all in it together, there was a certain pride and *esprit de corps* that accompanied the daily doing of our rounds.

In the lower ground floor of the main instruction building, there was a big chart, filling up an entire wall, outside the study hall. It was carefully drawn and gridded, with the jobs that rotated weekly. On Monday morning you got a number, studied the chart and the corresponding duty, and that was your new charge for the week. There were on the order of one hundred different jobs on "the Job Board."

Most of these corresponded to the actual place where the duty was to be done. "Upper floor, Boyd dorm." "Windows, 38 Dorm." There were five dorms, a gym, dining hall, faculty residences, infirmary, chapel, and assorted special-use spaces. "Yard duty, McCollough residence." The idea is sufficiently clear. One hundred jobs, 125 boys, farm duty.

There were also some permanent jobs, and you were lucky if you could get one. Some people just liked working at the farm, and these were jobs that didn't lend themselves to rotation. "The farm boys" liked wearing overalls, smoking, being around cows and chickens. They got to drive farm vehicles and be different. They did not incline to sports.

Another prized job was taking care of the many coal furnaces that brought the heat to numerous buildings on campus, and some faculty residences as well—if they'd not yet been converted to oil. This took a bit of basic training. The main thing was to know how and when to tend "the worm"—the aptly named device that fed coal into the furnace via turning a screw on an axle that ran from the coal bin and the furnace itself and conveyed the coal along. The coal being burned over some time left a hard, brittle deposit where the flame and blower conjoined, and would clog the worm if not removed. The technical term for this stuff was "a clinker." You deployed a long tool designed just for the task, removing the clinker ("the ash and partially fused residues from a coal-fired furnace") and depositing the hot, burned coal residue in a big bucket.

Failure properly to "tend the worm" fouled the crude but effective conveyance of coal, and activated a kill mechanism to prevent harming the furnace itself. It did happen, rarely. That flipped another kind of kill switch—kill the boy in charge of the furnace, who had let the dorms go cold. End of job. New recruits at the ready.

There were two great things about this job. You were on your own clock. The other jobs happened at the same time, twice every day, for a thirty-minute job period. It's pleasant to look at the poor, routinized comrades and smile wanly. The second thing: you could sneak a smoke. Down in your cozy, private, smelly furnace room, no one could smell a lit cigarette being hastily dropped in the clinker bucket when and if a faculty person popped in to "check on you." You had your own cloaking device, since the strong smell of coal effectively blocked out all lesser olfactory radar.

There were also big job days, once a week for four hours, for tackling major chores. Waxing the gym floor, mowing yards, painting gym lockers, relining the clay tennis courts.

And special assignments, issued at the discretion of the headmaster. A kind of papal office, in its day.

At Monday morning assembly, in the winter months, he would suddenly announce. "Coal car duty. Williams, Barnwell, Seitz, McIlhenny." It was a joy to have your name called out, as it would mean missing class. Instead, you put on nasty work clothes and a cap, gloves and shovels were issued, you jumped in the back of the truck assigned to this job, and you headed out to a siding off the local train line, where the coal train car was parked. Ordered, arrived, and ready to be shoveled into the truck's payload. Depending on how fast you worked, around five hours of hard labor.

I can recall how the next morning, your sides ached from unused muscles being put to work. Hard to turn the door handle. Raise your arms. Brush your teeth.

The headmaster wasn't just trying to save money. Obviously, others didn't get their coal in this unnecessarily arduous fashion. "I want you to appreciate that heat doesn't live in a radiator." "You don't turn on a switch and it drops in from outer space."

There is heat because people worked to bring it, and that includes you. Be economical with it.

―⁀―

I am writing this short preface to introduce my set of reflections on God as Creator, "Of all things, visible and invisible," as the Nicene Creed states it.

I do not start here merely or mainly as an exercise in nostalgia. The work program was not lots of fun and was not something one elected to do. Many students were shocked to realize they were signing on to something like this. Parents were cursed. Deals were considered. Schemes and bartering came to mind.

In a lot of ways, the work program was akin to the book of Leviticus. Let me explain. I'll start with a joke.

The gentiles invite a rabbi to explain to them the laws of Leviticus.

"They are about hygiene, right? Eat this, and you'll have better gut health."

The rabbi nods silently.

Another proposes, "They are about humanitarianism. 'Do not boil a kid in its mother's milk.'"

Again, a smile and signal of approval.

A third tries, "They are a symbol system pointing to higher truths."

The same approbation. The conference draws to a close.

The rabbi returns to his people, who have overheard the discussion.

"Do we believe these things, Rabbi?"

"No, they are answers I give to gentiles. We don't ask these questions. The laws are given to us because God loves us, and we do them to stay inside our life with Him."

The work program taught us something about obedience as having its own critical place in what it means to live life on its proper terms. Having jobs, over time, one loses a sense of oneself or the larger logic supposedly bigger than the simple need to live, to get on with what is expected, so the larger life of the school can flourish.

The French have an expression that is hard to translate. "Practice makes perfect" is offered, but it fails to get at what is being said.

C'est en forgeant, on devient forgeron.

You become a blacksmith by blacksmithing.

You burn your hand, create something misshapen, curse the wrong temperature of the kiln. This is obedience to a set of tasks and rules of the road that in turn make you someone.

It isn't so much the content or logic of laws that governs their utility and purpose. There could be five more or twenty-five less, and they would achieve the same thing. In the doing of the thing, we get remade. We learn there are things higher than us, that we need not fully understand for them to achieve what is needed. To interrogate the system is to move off the dance floor of life, where life is really lived.

And for the purpose of the book to follow, it is to live under God. This isn't asking a question about his metaphysical desirability, or to look down on the world he has made as he does. Not being able to do that is precisely what makes God, God. We shall have more to say about that as we go along.

The particular route I believe this requires us to go is to reflect on God as the Maker of heaven and earth. How, then, he descends from that place of standing to enter, love, and suffer the world he has made is the subject for another study. That said, we shall see its outlines as we go along, we who know the long story through the various angles of vision he has given us to glimpse him, in his majesty and in his condescension to us.

My particular concern, directing my thoughts in this project, is the loss of connection to the material world. "The sea is his for he made it, His hands prepared the dry land," are beginning to lose their meaning in any direct and moral and existential sense. They are words on a page, if we are prepared to give them utterance at all or ponder them.

We have fallen into cell phones. We cannot learn a route by letting our eyes and our memory do the work. So much cruelty and ghoulishness invade our consciousness, via flashing screens, their real form has lost any moral character. Walking a path, climbing a mountain, just trusting notches in trees—do we have the sensibility to do this, or has something short-circuited, and our bearings—our own relationship to the natural order—aren't able to bear anything in any direct and immediate way? Which is what our senses have been created to do.

I can feel the heft of a mattock in my hand, the same hand I am typing with as I follow words on the screen of a laptop popping up before my eyes. In my hand is a dying field dove, felled by a teenager helping clear them from the field corn. I pull the clogged, wet grass from the lawnmower's bag. I drop a hissing clinker into a pail, using the long awkward steel pincers. Treasures from a time close to nature and its ways.

Later I recall terror on the sea, because my navigational aid had been wrongly programmed. The squall was bad enough. But the grip in the stomach and the palpable dread were also increased due to my reliance on something without sense that stopped functioning. Sailors have known terrible dread from time immemorial. But their mastery of it arose from training their senses, knowing the price to be paid for placing oneself in the hands of him who rules the wind and waves, and soldiering on. There was nothing to be "fixed" that would lessen the requirement of living the real life under a real God whose laws are built into the world he has made. "The sea is his, for he made it."

He maketh not the GPS.

Part I
The Psalms of Creation

THE PSALMS AND THE MAJESTY OF GOD THE CREATOR

The heavens are telling the glory of God;
    and the firmament proclaims his handiwork.
Day to day pours forth speech,
    and night to night declares knowledge.
There is no speech, nor are there words;
    their voice is not heard;
yet their voice goes out through all the earth,
    and their words to the end of the world. (Ps 19:1–4)

In my parish church, a small group gathers during the week to read Morning Prayer together.

It may be hard for many people to recall that, not long ago, Morning Prayer was the principal Sunday morning service in the Anglican tradition. A new prayer book, and some converging ecumenical thinking, sought to make Holy Communion the regular Sunday rite. There are obvious things to be said in favor of that. In my part of the Christian world, the Eucharist has been celebrated with rare exception as the principal Sunday service since the late 1970s. Over fifty years now. Morning Prayer is the domain of weekday services at seminaries, and the occasional parish church.

One of the things that strikes me now is how much of Morning Prayer (and the daily offices in general) is praise of God for his own sake. And that means praise of him as Creator of the world around us. "For he is our God, and we are the people of his pasture, and the sheep of his hand." "Let all the inhabitants of the world stand in awe of him." "Glory to you beholding the depths, in the high vault of heaven, glory to you." "In his hand are the depths of the earth; the heights of the hills are his also. The sea is his, for he made it; for his hands formed the dry land."

These are for the most part lines straight from the Psalms or participating in their same scale and worldview. What is a high vault of heaven, or even more so, what does it mean to praise God beholding the depths? We can get used to this soaring language but if we pause to ask what is being described, we must enter the cosmic, creational, primordial realms of God himself.

"Deep calls to deep," the psalm intones, "at the thunder of thy cataracts." What is a cataract and what does it mean to say "thy waves and thy billows have gone over me," while God himself "sits enthroned over the flood"?

Now there are answers to these questions. The images from nature are what they are, while at the same time they describe our own fragile creaturely condition, over against them. God is majestic. We are not. The Psalms delight in holding up this majesty and authority, and they ask us to reside in its powerful shade. We shall have occasion to see this in quite dramatic and unparalleled form in the book of Job, and specifically in the divine responses to the man Job.

When God answers Job, the curious thing is that he offers no explanation. No discourses on why horrible things befall the faithful. No sympathetic or therapeutic words of condolence. Instead, he lets creation speak. In all its manifold, exotic, dangerous, and concrete materiality. As one interpreter comments, "As God says of Himself what He does say in His speeches, and as Job allows to be said to him what he may and must allow to be said, he is put in his place by God, and yet, because it is God who does this, he is put in a good place."

The Psalms do this in a more generalized way, throughout the 150-leg journey that constitutes the Psalter as it comes to us.

The opening verses of Psalm 19 are particularly significant when it comes to our theme, and I choose to begin here because of this. The paradoxical nature of creation having no vocal cords, but nevertheless capable of rich speech, is how the psalm opens.

> Day to day pours forth speech,
>   and night to night declares knowledge. (19:2)

The regular movement of the day to day, and of the night to night, "speaks." This march of time makes its voice heard, because God is the agent of the mysterious, grand regularity we witness each day of our lives.

The psalm continues:

> There is no speech, nor are there words;
>   their voice is not heard;
> yet their voice goes out through all the earth,
>   and their words to the end of the world. (19:3–4)

And here there is the acknowledgment, the recognition, that this speaking forth happens without the words that we creatures, made in God's image, use to communicate. And the scope and scale of this raised "voice" goes to the very ends of the world, wherever day and night are experienced—which is to say, everywhere in God's creation. Where we are, and where we are not. We do not have to be present to "hear" this regular changing of day to night for that same changing to speak forth.

We are used to thinking of creation as at least potentially noisy. Thunderclap. Falling rain. Even the more silent snow as it passes through the atmosphere and falls to the ground. The singing of birds and of the sea. The crashing of waves, or the noise of falling debris when weather and time and gravity conspire to force subsidence. The blowing of the dolphin, the breaching of the whale. Even the dramatic lightning bolt seems paired to the thunder that follows it, and so with its own silent sound. "There is no speech, nor are there words, yet their voice goes out through all the earth."

God's grandeur in creation is talking to us. Made in his image, he asks us to listen.

Psalm 29

The voice of the Lord is upon the waters;
   the God of glory thunders,
   the Lord, upon many waters.
The voice of the Lord is powerful,
   the voice of the Lord is full of majesty.
The Lord sits enthroned over the flood; . . .
   the Lord sits enthroned as king forever. (Ps 29:3–4, 10)

In the beginning, at the dawn of creation, there was "chaos and void"—the Hebrew word *tohuwabohu* so traditionally translated.

God spoke, and the chaos and void were tamed. He began creating. Light, heavens and earth, sun, moon, stars, herbage, creatures of air, earth, and sea. Finally, those made in his image, who see the wonders of creation and more, are given to understand that they are God's.

But chaos isn't "back there." Creation isn't "back there." The psalmist knows that chaos is here and now, in the upheavals of life, in the floods that reach up to our neck and threaten to overwhelm us.

God once flooded the entire good world he had made, and those made in his image, who distorted themselves and God and creation, were swept up into its waters. He un-created. Instead of "let there be" he brought on "let there not be."

And the rainbow we see now in the skies is the formal agreement, the surety, that he will not do that on that scale again, until the curtain of time is drawn down and a new heaven and earth arise at his hand.

What is he doing now? The psalmist answers: he is sitting enthroned above the flood. The waters are held back behind the firmament of heaven and below the earth's surface. There he sits, a bulwark, a strong tower, the Creator holding chaos and void in his firm hand. The psalmist in another place will rejoice at the firm regularity by which God sovereignly rules the world he has made, the heavens and the sea.

> In [the heavens] he has set a tent for the sun,
> which comes forth like a bridegroom leaving his chamber,
>   and like a strong man runs its course with joy.
> Its rising is from the end of the heavens,
>   and its circuit to the end of them;
>   and there is nothing hid from its heat. (Ps 19:4–6)

We hear the same notes in the preface to Ecclesiastes. Like the child kicking his chair, saying, "do it again, do it again," the endless regular repetition that keeps us alive and well proceeds of itself, at God's command.

> A generation goes, and a generation comes,
>   but the earth remains forever.
> The sun rises and the sun goes down,
>   and hastens to the place where it rises.
> The wind blows to the south,
>   and goes round to the north;
> round and round goes the wind,
>   and on its circuits the wind returns.
> All streams run to the sea,
>   but the sea is not full;
> to the place where the streams flow,
>   there they flow again. (Eccl 1:4–7)

In the words of Hemingway, measured against the folly and vanity of human conduct, "The sun also rises." It does this tirelessly, eternally. The wind does not blow itself out. The seas are governed and ruled, so they may flood and ebb, but their courses are under God's final control. "He sits enthroned above the flood."

In this psalm, it is the voice of God, rather than the voice of creation, that is the poet's focus.

> The voice of the LORD is upon the waters;
>> the God of glory thunders,
>> the LORD, upon many waters.
> The voice of the LORD is powerful;
>> the voice of the LORD is full of majesty. (Ps 29:3–4)

One may suppose that the creation account is being referenced here. God speaks the world into being. "And he said, and so it was." The voice that spoke once at creation's inauguration continues to speak. God's creative work is continual. He is keeping the world on its course, he is speaking over the waters he holds under his control, and his voice is powerful, majestic, more thunderous than the thunder he dispatches in storms.

We pay a lot of attention to disruptions in the "natural order." TV stations alert us to hurricanes, volcanic eruptions, weather patterns bringing change and warning, high tides, tsunamis, blizzards, ice storms, high winds. What we fail to take into consciousness is the will of God active in daily creation, creating the stable, regular conditions whose disruptions give us pause or fear. God is enthroned above the flood. He is "moving" the sun across the heavens by making the earth rotate flawlessly and regularly. Our watches work. We can "tell time." The tide chart knows what it's doing. After a nor'easter the seas at last flatten over their huge rollers, until even they calmly recede back to the usual deportment of their daily life.

And so we glimpse through raging storms and gale the psalmist's "deep speaks to deep at the thunder of their cataracts," before the wonted rest returns and the ship sails on, sure that the Creator's world is solid and in good hands, even at sea. "The sea is his, for he made it."

"Who is this, that even the wind and waves obey his voice?" As of Father, so of Son. "The voice of the LORD is powerful. The voice of the LORD is majestic."

Psalms double back and reinforce. Here is the psalm numbered by us "93."

> The LORD reigns; he is robed in majesty;
>   the LORD is robed, he is girded with strength.
> Yea, the world is established; it shall never be moved;
>   thy throne is established from of old;
>   thou art from everlasting.
>
> The floods have lifted up, O LORD,
>   the floods have lifted up their voice,
>   the floods lift up their roaring.
> Mightier than the thunders of many waters,
>   mightier than the waves of the sea,
>   the LORD on high is mighty! (Ps 93:1–4)

Let it be a coda on this reflection, God, above the flood, magnificent in authority. King of the creation that loves him and that does his full bidding.

Psalms 46 and 69

God is our refuge and strength,
    a very present help in trouble.
Therefore we will not fear though the earth should change,
    though the mountains shake in the heart of the sea,
though its waters roar and foam,
    though the mountains tremble with its tumult. (Ps 46:1–3)

Save me, O God!
    For the waters have come up to my neck.
I sink in deep mire,
    where there is no foothold;
I have come into deep waters,
    and the flood sweeps over me.
        . . .
Let not the flood sweep over me,
    or the deep swallow me up,
    or the pit close its mouth over me.
Answer me, LORD, for thy steadfast love is good;
    according to thy abundant mercy, turn to me.
        . . .
The LORD hears the needy,
    and does not despise his own that are in bonds.
Let heaven and earth praise him,
    the seas and everything that moves therein.
        (Ps 69:1–2, 15–16, 33–34)

Psalm 46 lets us know that the ordered and faithfully regulated created order can also burst its bounds. The psalmist allows us to see this reality. Should the earth give way, if the mountains were to fall into the sea, there stands God. "The God of Jacob is our refuge and our strength." Reading on, we hear the repeated refrain. "Be still and know that I am God."

A wise author says this about waiting during times of darkness and a sense that the world is crashing around us.

"He makes us wait. He keeps us on purpose in the dark. He makes us walk when we want to run, sit still when we want to walk, for He has things to do in our souls that we are not interested in."

There is no word for "spirituality" in the Old Testament. The Psalms speak of the discipline of waiting. That is its concrete form of "spirituality." "Be still and know that I am God" belongs in this register.

The pain of wanting, needing, missing is the forge on which God reshapes us so we can receive what he has to say. And that forge is hard and the reshaping painful.

Psalm 69 gives a more concrete picture of what it is like to feel the world falling apart around us. We cannot find a foothold. The waters are up to our necks. The depths that God holds in reserve, the flood over which he sits enthroned—there are times in life where we sense we are drowning. We cannot be still and know that God is God, because we are scared, and the fear focuses our mind just there. All we can do—the psalmist knows this—is to cry out, "Save me."

And so, the psalm gives voice to just these times in life. No platitudes. No secret passageways. No narcotic. No well-meaning counselor. It is about God and me. You. Us. These other things may come alongside, or we may dream them up out of desperation, but at its root, our cry is to God and God alone.

Do not let me drown. Do not let the pit cover me. Do not let me keep sinking and feel it will go on and on, without a floor to hit.

The one who rules the sky and sea, who preparest the dry land—our cry is to him. Even when the words are more like gasping for air. We know that the air, the spirit he breathed into us and that now cries out, is calling out to the one who is the giver of life and breath. "Answer me."

There is a ground for this appeal that is coming into frame. The goodness of God. The cry makes its appeal here. "God" is not a name uttered in sheer desperation, without content. God is goodness. God is mercy. He does not despise. His eye is precisely on the needy. The poor in spirit, they are those who know their need of God, and who know that God is goodness and mercy. He can be called upon as he is.

And here, in the mystery of his timing, of his appearing, of his showing himself good and merciful, our equilibrium is restored. The good world of his superintending and divine regulating is called upon to praise him who made them.

> Let heaven and earth praise him,
>> the seas and everything that moves therein.

How it is that this journey from utter desperation and drowning and raw fear becomes instead a cry directed to the God of goodness belongs to a path no man can know. One finds oneself on this path—it arises unbidden in life, occasioned by so many different challenges, including finally death itself—and within the household of God and a life lived with him, it will unfold in ways known to him alone, with a timing his own. The psalmist describes this path because he knows it, and he shares it from the inside out.

For us, the psalmists that we too are, it will come with its own signature. At his timing. With his presence in the deep. With, as he wills it, his goodness and mercy.

PSALMS 93 AND 96

I had to take my vintage sailboat, hull #1, on a nine-hour voyage up the Intracoastal Waterway, inside the Atlantic coastline, in South Carolina. The trip got postponed a day and I was under time pressure, so the trip had to go forward.

I have been on boats with heavier and worse weather, but it rained very hard. Soaked to the core. Shiveringly bone-wet. On the water, the visibility can be very poor under such conditions. It was. I was helped by my sailing friend's eyes and his shared time at the helm. The boat has a navigational device, and on that voyage, it was very helpful.

The three-thousand-mile Intracoastal, begun in the late nineteenth century, was constructed by the Army Corps of Engineers and it was quite a feat, much like the earlier canal systems in France. For the most part, advantage is taken of rivers and bodies of water already carved out by the hand of God. But need arises at certain junctures for cuts made by human hand and heavy machinery. Narrow dredged canals link bodies of water already in place. Some can be very long (North Carolina/Virginia border), even requiring locks. For this reason, seasoned travelers and passage makers (Florida to Maine) refer to the waterway as "the ditch."

In France, where changes in elevation and deep valleys must be negotiated, locks are omnipresent. One can even experience vast bridge expanses made just for the canal boat traffic. There is something whimsical about moving slowly along in your craft, high above the landscape below, nestled in a canal of concrete, supported by grand arches underneath. There you are, moving by water, in the air high above the ground below.

You can have something of the reverse sensation when the fog is extremely dense, enabling you to barely see the bow of your craft, as you pass under a vast bridge overhead. Seeing nothing, slowly you make out the huge pylons at your side, while above your head, high above, cars and trucks clamber along. Tires whirring, horns sounding. You cannot see them, but you sense the height of the huge bridge you are passing under. The south end of Manhattan Island is a good example.

All this comes at you as remarkable human endeavor, made possible by the Industrial Revolution and the invention of heavy diesel machinery, now centuries in the rearview mirror. We now take that for granted. Yet, on the occasions I am noting here, you sense immediately the sheer height and depth and scale of this Revolution, because you are in the same craft men have used from time immemorial. A boat. A sail. A rudder.

From Denmark, to England, down the coast of France, along the massive rivers, the Seine, the Rhine, the Rhone and Saone, into the Mediterranean, and on and on. A rope with knots at intervals, trailing behind the boat, indicating the same six knots displayed on my modern GPS, while today the vast network and inventions of modernity speed along their busy way, above, below, and beside you. A time warp, as it were. Fit to remind you of our modest place in the world. Of the grand scale of things.

This is all but a shadow of the world of the psalmist. The world of God he beholds and is given by God to see.

> The LORD reigns; he is robed in majesty;
>> the LORD is robed, he is girded with strength.
> Yea, the world is established; it shall never be moved;
>> thy throne is established from of old;
>> thou art from everlasting.
>
> The floods have lifted up, O LORD,
>> the floods have lifted up their voice,
>> the floods lift up their roaring.

> Mightier than the thunders of many waters,
>> mightier than the waves of the sea,
>> the LORD on high is mighty! (Ps 93:1–4)

The psalmist can see the manner in which the grand scale of creation amounts to a kind of dangerous power and raw authority. "Robed in dreadful majesty" is God Almighty. The created world is so vast and so apparently poised to break its bounds, as it does what it does and is what it is, the psalmist must allow its voice to arise, and that reality to speak for itself.

But solely in the name of ascribing it all to God, whose throne is from eternity and whose own hand made the world we see and abide in. With all its thundering power. The sea can be an unruly and overwhelming place, and sailors enter it with proper trepidation and are awed before its might. "The sea is his, and he made it."

Yet for he who made it, the psalmist also sees a kind of divine pride, a joyful love of its wild exuberance. God making the whale for fun, for his pleasure. "There go the ships, and Leviathan which thou didst form to sport in it," the psalmist proclaims. Let creation raise its voice.

> Let the sea roar, and all that fills it;
>> the world and those who dwell in it!
> Let the floods clap their hands;
>> let the hills sing for joy together. (Ps 98:7–8)

Hebrew poetry is so designated for one main thing: it must say one thing, turn and look at it, and say it again. In speaking of God and his ways, a superabundance, as Donne put it, rules. X, yea, Y.

So, we make our way along in our tiny boat, measured by the scale of God's world, where he pulls the tides and then releases them. Again and again and again, from his eternal throne. Never to be altered, always the same. "Do it again, do it again." Happily, says the psalmist, and while you are at it, clap your hands. God likes to see that. He rejoices in the world he has made, and it sings back his praises.

The Tides of the Psalter

A sailboat has a maximal speed at which it can move through the water. A simple formula based on the length of the waterline (not boat length overall) dictates the speed of the boat—what is called its "hull speed." This is for the simple reason that a sailboat cannot "plane"—that is, cannot exit the wake it pushes in front of it as it moves along.

A powerboat, on the other hand, has an auxiliary feature—the high-powered motor—that enables the boat to escape its wake. Powerboaters know this, and it is easily enough understood. They throttle the motor at a high enough level that the boat lifts itself over the wake it is pushing, and then it calms down and the speed can be set back, then increased as one wishes.

This is precisely the same thing we mean when we speak of "breaking the sound barrier." A modern jet airplane will have a maximal speed (much like the sailboat; not six knots, but nearly six hundred). It would need to "escape its own wake" via super-sonic thrust (the Concorde could do it, and other supersonic craft). When this happens, there is turbulence, shaking, and then calm, following the "boom" we hear below.

To make the point a bit clearer: I flew back and forth between Glasgow or Edinburgh and the United States for a decade, six to ten times a year. Leaving the United States and flying east-ward across the north Atlantic, you were on a flight path—the Great Circle—that all planes took. Whether headed to Glasgow, London, or Amsterdam, you followed the same arc in the sky. The

Boeing (or comparable) jet-engine-powered aircraft left clean vapor trails, and each jet within that species flew within five to ten miles per hour more or less than the others. It would take perhaps an hour or so, to be overtaken by or to overtake, slowly but surely, planes on the same route. At the top of the world, the sun coming up, you could glimpse the majesty of the created arc of the world, and human engineering quietly humming along. Your vapor trail close alongside another, in the snowy clean sky stretching out before you.

Unlike the airplane, boats—this is especially so in the rivers of South Carolina and elsewhere—are subject to tides. Tides can reach speeds of six knots and more, depending on the waterways and intervening rivers and bays and creeks. So, the sailboat is at the mercy of these. My boat, for example, can only do as much as four knots when the tide is running at full throttle in my face. The auxiliary engine is giving it all it has got, not pushing the boat across its wake as with the powerboat, but pushing as hard as it can against this inrushing effect.

And of course, happily, the opposite is true when the tide is your friend and your boat is traveling inside its joyful rush forward. The boat stays within its bounds due to hull speed but gets this lovely speed increase because it is riding along with the tide.

This means that on a twelve-hour journey on the Eastern Seaboard, where there are two tides a day, you get a perfect mixture of being slowed down and being lifted along, in equal portions.

This mirrors the life we live "under the sun," to quote the Preacher of Ecclesiastes. There is a time for embracing, and a time to refrain from embracing. For living, and finally, for dying. You will know its wise refrain, even popularized by the Byrds and others. "To everything, turn, turn, turn, there is a season, turn, turn, turn." One of those few occasions where the Bible is not ruined by popularizations.

Life has valleys, and mountaintops, and this admixture teaches us to see joy as a gift, even more so after a storm or deep valley. The valley of the shadow of death, and the table set before us where our cup overflows. Where finally, on the day known by God, we go to dwell in the House of the LORD forevermore. When God calls us who love him home.

The Psalter comes to us in the form of five books. In the first three, David and the monarchy are the dominant protagonists. There are also many psalms without attribution. One can well imagine David as a man of prayer and music, becoming the inspiration for kindred prayers rising up within the household of faith.

David is a man of prayer, of praise, and of lament. The promises made to him are set out right at the beginning (Ps 2), as well as for his sons who will follow him. God will protect David. Those who arise against him will be put to shame. God looks down from heaven and holds them in derision. This means that as enemies arise to threaten him, his sons, and God's people Israel, this is transpiring against the bulwark of God's sure and true promises.

We have been looking at the form these take quite specifically in the natural order, God's creation, with him enthroned above the flood. The seas lift up their voice; the cataracts roar; the earth trembles around us. We are reminded: "Be still, and know that I am God." The voice of the LORD is mightier than anything in creation. The wind and waves obey him.

It is this majestic authority undergirding what David and Israel are experiencing in their journey through time, assaulted by enemies, assaulted by the effects of sin, assaulted by doubts rising up, broken and crying out for help. Sometimes, in fact quite often, asking simply, "Are you there? Why are you hiding your face? Why is my soul so disquieted within me?" This serves as a mirror of our own journey of faith, seeking God's face, asking why the lights have gone out, not sure there is a foothold in the pit, waters rising up to our neck.

The refrains which serve to mark the beginning and ending of these first three books (and the last two) never change, however, in spite of the ups and downs, the valleys and the mountain tops where our glimpse at God's majesty and faithfulness is partial but always soaring—a foretaste of seeing Him face to face. A beholding consistent with life on earth, in some sense protecting us from seeing the full glory of his eternal love, before its proper time, which here would amount to overwhelming Light.

These refrains are nearly carbon copies of each other. We appreciate the role they play on behalf of the Psalter as a whole, and the journey of David and Israel from the founding of the monarchy to the exile, because the psalms for which they form the conclusion (Pss 41, 73, 89, 106, and 150) in fact have their own obvious endings. The refrains are independent and sometimes the typesetting of English Bible translations will choose to capture this.

One can see this easily enough by quick reference. For example, Psalm 41 concludes, "But thou hast upheld me because of my integrity, and set me in thy presence forever." There then follows, "Blessed be the LORD, the God of Israel, from everlasting to everlasting! Amen and Amen." Note the similarity, even extended in form, at the end of Psalm 72. "Blessed be the LORD, the God of Israel, who alone does wondrous things. Blessed be his glorious name for ever; may his glory fill the whole earth! Amen and Amen" (vv. 18, 19). The obvious ending of Psalm 72 comes in verse 17, which precedes this. As if to underscore the function of the refrains in the context of the whole Psalter, after the refrain concluding Book Two, an editor has added, "The prayers of David, the son of Jesse, are ended" (v. 20).

In Book Three (Pss 73–89), a much shorter section of the Psalter, we find psalms attributed to choral guilds (Asaph, Korah) or otherwise obscure figures (Ethan the Ezrahite, Ps 89). David appears in attribution in Psalm 86 alone. This is a prayer for mercy recalling God's faithfulness in the past and pleading to him on that basis.

The final psalm (89) clearly has the man David, and the entire lineage given to him in promised covenant relationship (2 Sam 7), in view. The promise is explicitly recalled at the psalm's opening (Ps 89:1–4) and in an extended poetic section at the middle of the psalm (vv. 19–37). The verses intervening (vv. 5–18) situate themselves alongside the theme we are pursuing here: God's majesty and authority over the created world of his making. His defeat of chaos. His ruling of winds and waves.

This is important to note. God's rule over the created order, like creation itself, has a stunning priority. We may tend, in reading the Old Testament, to think of God's acts. His election of Israel and the unfolding drama of his life with them. The patriarchs, Promised Land, the covenant with David, the history reported in the books of Samuel, Kings, and Chronicles. Exile and return. Somehow to be fitted alongside this dominant narrative line, the wisdom books (Psalms, Job, Proverbs, Ecclesiastes).

But God made a covenant with creation. He placed a rainbow in the sky. It is this created order and rule that allow history to be history at all. "Time is in his hand." We can even see this prioritization at points in the prophets, where the wheels of history appear to have come off, and the tide of God's ebbing life with his people has receded all the way out, to the point of total death and dryness.

Jeremiah's promise of a new covenant (Jer 31:31–34) is grounded in God the Creator, "who gives the sun for light by day and the fixed order of the moon and the stars for light by night, who stirs up the sea so that its waves roar—the LORD of hosts is his name" (v. 35). Jeremiah swears that if this fixed order were to depart, his people would cease, with the oath-form implication: the descendants of Israel shall never experience such an ultimate fate.

In Isaiah we see a similar deep prioritization. Speaking to the dead bones of an exiled people, whose historical and existential compass is broken, he says:

> "For this is like the days of Noah to me:
>   as I swore that the waters of Noah
>   should no more go over the earth,
> so I have sworn that I will not be angry with you
>   and will not rebuke you.
> For the mountains may depart
>   and the hills be removed,
> but my steadfast love shall not depart from you,

> and my covenant of peace shall not be removed,
> says the LORD, who has compassion on you."
> (Isa 54:9–10)

This is exactly the same direction that Psalm 89, the final psalm of Book Three, takes. The majestic authority of God over chaos and the forces of creation is set alongside his promises to David at the start. Then the covenant with David, as mighty in character as God the Creator, is recalled. The two themes sit side by side as this section of the psalm concludes.

> Once for all I have sworn by my holiness;
>   I will not lie to David.
> His line shall endure for ever,
>   his throne as long as the sun before me.
> Like the moon it shall be established for ever;
>   it shall stand firm while the skies endure. (Ps 89:35–37)

Then we come to a characteristic, clearly disjunctive transition, which enforces the verticality of God and his sovereignty over what we would imagine to be the correct narrative sequencing, according to our limited instincts about how the storyline of life ought to play out.

> But now thou hast cast off and rejected,
>   thou art full of wrath against thy anointed. (89:38)

The entire solid bulwark of creation and the one enthroned over the flood, the same one who pledged an eternal covenant to David and his lineage and the sure history of his people whom he loves—gone. The tide that would run out for Israel in Books One through Three, and that would flow back again in accordance with God's creational authority, has seemingly stopped its "again and again" movement on the historical plane. The remainder of the psalm (vv. 39–51) simply describes this heartbreaking reality and the anguish it occasions. The only thing left is lament and the cry for God to recall what he has promised.

And to ask the burning question we reviewed in Psalms 46 and 69 above, in the case of the individual. Now not the individual with waters reaching to the neck and no foothold, however, but the whole history of God with his entire people. A timeline broken. The tide of God's ebbing and flowing has flooded back and has drowned his people. From the depths we are given to hear the cry, "How long?" "Remember what you promised." "David, the man of 'for the sake of David,' look at his plight, how they mock the footsteps of your anointed."

The final refrain will still be spoken, as at the close of Books One and Two, now compressed, a reminder to God all the same, "Blessed be the LORD forever! Amen and Amen." The "out of the depths, I cry to you; LORD, hear my prayer" in the form of a simple doxology of hope and praise.

For that psalm (130), we must now wait.

William Blake (1757–1827), "Mercy and Truth Are Met Together,
Righteousness and Peace Have Kissed Each Other."
Victoria & Albert Museum, London, UK/Bridgeman Images.

William Blake (1757–1827), "The Ascension," ca. 1805–1806. Pen, pencil, indian ink, and watercolor. Fitzwilliam Museum, University of Cambridge, UK. Photo © Fitzwilliam Museum/Bridgeman Images.

William Blake (1757–1827), "David Delivered out of Many Waters,"
ca. 1805. Ink and watercolor on paper. Acquisition presented by
George Thomas Saul, 1878. Tate Gallery, London, Great Britain.
Photo © Tate, London/Art Resource, New York.

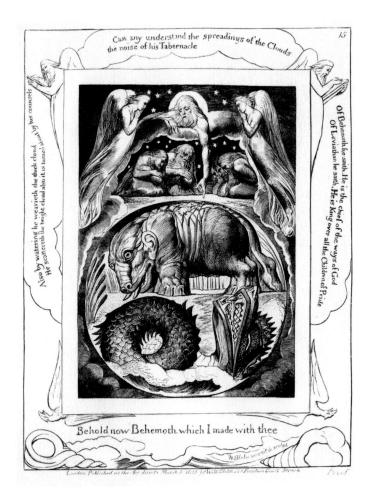

William Blake (1757–1827), "The Book of Job 40:15 & 41:34,"
illustration from *The Book of Job*, first published 1826.
Photo by Lebrecht Authors/Bridgeman Images.

William Blake (1757–1827), "The Book of Job 38:1–2,"
first published 1826. Photo by Lebrecht Authors/Bridgeman Images.

William Blake (1757–1827), "The Book of Job 42:8,"
first published 1826. Photo by Lebrecht Authors/Bridgeman Images.

Book Four of the Psalter

We all of us know times when the lights go out. Darkness and no storyline we can follow. When, with the song writer, we ask, "Am I a prisoner of hope, or just the warden of my pain? My head knows to trust you, but this heart of mine is slain."

I was at my wife's bedside as she died of Covid. A darkness made more severe because a lung transplant in Paris restored her to me, only four short years earlier, after she had suffered the ravages of a rare pulmonary condition.

The way the darkness makes itself felt is physically like torture. The pain sears. It lasts. It seems to subside and then it comes again in massive force, for reasons one cannot know. "When you lose someone you love, your life becomes strange, the ground beneath you becomes fragile," a poet describes it. "Suddenly without warning, you are ambushed by grief." "You are thrown back on the black tide of loss."

> Sorrow will remain faithful to itself.
> More than you, it knows its way
> And will find the right time
> To pull and pull the rope of grief
> Until the coiled hill of tears
> Has reduced to its last drop
>
> To wean your eyes
> From that gap in the air
> And be able to enter the hearth
> In your soul where your loved one
> Has awaited your return
> All the time.

None of this has a script. It refuses to be so tamed. God can only be called on, cried to, begged upon in heartbroken petition to "restore our fortunes, like the waters of the Negev." May the dealings of your hand be kind again. God, let the black tide become again the tide of your grace, joy, and hope. God, help.

Where now is David? Where are the people crying out in the darkness of despair, as the worst thing imaginable arrives: the loss of God, his face hidden, his journey with us gone?

As we cross the border into Book Four, Moses appears, that great intercessor who laid his own life on the line so as to stay God's judgment and preserve the relationship he promised to have with his people forever. The covenant with David cast down. The covenant with Moses appealed to. The appeal of Moses himself, reminding God of his solemn promises to the patriarchs. "Make us glad as many days as thou hast afflicted us." Let the tides ebb and flow again. "Let the favor of the LORD be upon us again."

The sixteen psalms of Book Four are content for the most part to arise without ascription. One psalm begins simply, "The LORD reigns" (93), and changes on this theme are a distinctive feature of the Book. "The LORD is a great God, and a great King above all gods"—the psalm that gives the title for this present book (95). "Say among the nations, 'The LORD reigns'" (96:10). "The LORD reigns, let the earth rejoice" (97:1). "Make a joyful noise before the King, the LORD" (98:6). "The LORD reigns; let the peoples tremble" (99:1). "Thou, O LORD, art enthroned for ever" (102:12).

Behind and undergirding David the king, God is King. He reigns. His throne is secure. There is a river whose streams make glad the city of God. God is in the midst of her. She shall not be moved. Let the nations tremble. Slowly but surely the notes of prior psalms begin to arrive. And in the middle of Book Four, psalms ascribed to David resurface twice (101 and 103). In between them, we have a fitting title, "a prayer of one afflicted, when he is faint and pours out his complaint before the LORD"

(102). Well, that says it all. David, you go first, I'll follow, and you can speak again.

"I will sing of loyalty and of justice; to thee, O LORD, I will sing" (101:1) David's voice is coming back. "Bless the LORD, O my soul; and all that is within me, bless his holy name" (103:1). And beginning to soar again. "Who forgives all your iniquity" (103:3). Sharing what he has to say in a first-person plural fellowship. "As a father pities his children, so the LORD pities those who fear him" (103:13).

> For he knows our frame
> He remembers that we are dust. (103:14)

The very first action of God toward us, his personal spirit blown into our lungs that starts the cycle of birth down all generations, including the French lungs bringing breath to my wife. He formed man from the dust. Remember you are dust and to dust you shall return. God remembers, in love, the frailty of our condition. The dust out of which we were formed and life blown into us by the very spirit/breath (the same word in Hebrew) of God the Creator.

> When thou hidest thy face, they are dismayed
>   when thou takest away their breath, they die
>   and return to their dust.
> When thou sendest forth thy Spirit, they are created;
>   and thou renewest the face of the ground. (104:29–30)

The voice of the anonymous afflicted one sums up this Book Four well.

> Let this be recorded for a generation to come,
>   so that a people yet unborn may praise the LORD:
> That he looked down from his holy height,
>   from heaven the LORD looked at the earth,
> To hear the groans of prisoners,
>   to set free those who were doomed to die. (102:18–20)

The words of our poet,

> Sorrow will remain faithful to itself.
> More than you, it knows its way
> And will find the right time.

Will find the right time. God has our times in his hand. The tides go out and sometimes they flow back and drown us, and we can only cry out to him to speak and restore and be God again as we knew him.

This is also likely why another feature of Book Four and the season it represents, mirroring the seasons of our life, can be found at the end of it. Psalms 105 and 106 tell the long and candid story of God's faithfulness in the past. Sometimes in seasons of exile and darkness, we have to turn to what we know to be true about God's ways as we have experienced them in the past. We pull the album down from the shelf. We dust off the photos. We come alongside the past he gave us, and that he shared with us, and we let its details remind us of his goodness and mercy.

In the exodus, God showed himself mighty. "He led forth his people in joy, his chosen ones with singing. . . . Praise the LORD!" (105:43, 45) is the ending crescendo of the long forty-five-verse recital of God's faithfulness in time and space, his concrete life with the people he longed to deliver. And did.

There is even remembrance of failure and disobedience, the flip side of the more positive portrayal in Psalm 105, such as we find it in the forty-seven-verse Psalm 106 to follow. Oddly enough, though we must be reminded of it, failure in relationship is still relationship. God with his people. The psalmist evokes this track record not to humiliate but as the grounds for coming alongside a people similarly in the straits of judgment.

> Save us, O LORD our God
>> and gather us from among the nations (as once you did)
> that we may give thanks to thy holy name
>> and glory in thy praise (now in our day).
>>> (106:47, parenthetical comments added)

And with that final word of Book Four, we come up again before the fourth refrain in the series previously noted. It seems to be especially suited to its position following the content of Book Four as a whole, and the end of its concluding psalm.

Blessed be the LORD, the God of Israel,
> From everlasting to everlasting!
And let the people say, "Amen!"
> Praise the LORD! (106:48)

Israel stricken, in anguish, in darkness, God's face hidden for a season. Then her voice returns once more. To bless God, who took away, and who gives again. Again and again, the tides back on course. And let the people say, "Amen!"

Amen.

THE MAJESTY OF
GOD IN CREATION

The songwriter who in the previous chapter spoke about the pain and darkness inside the slain heart, will finally be moved to say, "Faithful LORD, the dealings of your hand." And "Faithful LORD, the tides pulled by your hand."

Tides are returning to their eternal "again and again" in Book Four. The distinctive features of this section of the Psalter have been noted. Moses. The LORD is King. The voice of David rising and gaining strength. The albums of the "dealings of your hand" that Israel opens, reminding her of the details of the past journey with God—the joyful deliverances as well as moments of failure and rebellion. These together constitute life under God. In the recollection of conduct that she allows to arise, there is the acknowledgment of the present season of judgment and darkness. She calls for help and for the white tide of God's returning love and faithfulness.

Now we can return more centrally to the theme of the present book: the majesty of God in creation.

The psalms and canticles of Morning Prayer referred to in the opening chapter belong to this portion of the Psalter. The Venite. What the annotation of my Bible calls, "Psalm 95: A Liturgy of God's Kingship." The Prayer Book's Venite comes from the words with which the psalm opens, "O come, let us sing to the LORD." And the portion we are using to organize our treatment:

> In his hand are the corners of the earth;
>   the heights of the hills are his also.

The sea is his, for he made it;
    and his hand prepared the dry land. (Ps 95:4–5)

In the standard Morning Prayer service, the Venite is joined by the Jubilate (Psalm 100). Inside the organization of the Psalter, Psalm 100 has often been considered the doxology of the preceding songs praising God as king.

Be joyful in the LORD, all you lands;
. . .
Know this: the LORD himself is God.

The first line's exhortation to be joyful is where the shortened Latin title, Jubilate, gets its name: "O be joyful."

When the series of covenants—solemn declarations of commitment—begin to topple for a season (covenants with the patriarchs, with Moses, with David), God stands in the creation he has made and declares that here, he is the strong tower holding all things together, including the people he has made for himself.

The psalmist is given to see this bedrock of God's majesty, undergirding all things, the source of faith, hope, and the restoring of fortune (*shuv shevut*, in Hebrew). "When the LORD restored the fortunes of Zion, we were like those who dream" (Ps 126:1). The language used here has been carefully chosen. It is not a matter of conjuring up, by force of will, a determination that all must be well. The dream arises in the night, unbidden, the conjugation of bits of memory and passing thought, given by God's hand for just this season, so as to display his majesty and loving-kindness. A ray of light piercing the darkness, the gift of hope, the unforeseen horizon of returning love.

In the midst of darkness, the prophet Jeremiah sees a Promised Land arise, as did Moses, his mentor and model. He says, "I awoke and looked, and my sleep was pleasant to me" (Jer 31:26). There will be a future. "For I know the plans I have for you, says the LORD, plans for welfare and not for evil, to give you a future and a hope" (29:11). To bring you home, secure in the world I have made and that I uphold.

How fitting, then, that here Psalm 104 raises its voice. In coming sections, we will look at God's address to Job in chapters 38–41, after he has suffered an ordeal predicated precisely for him and only for him because of his unparalleled righteousness and unique relationship with God. Psalm 104 is the closest thing we have to those speeches, given for a different, later season of corporate darkness and exile.

Up to this point it has served my purposes to work with extracts of psalms from Books One through Three, to illustrate aspects of God the Creator I have wanted to highlight. It is important, here, at this juncture, to let the whole psalm—unlike anything we have seen thus far—stand as it is. One can sense the global picture it gives just by watching it unfold in its marvelous details and beams of light.

In the creation account itself, in the opening chapter of the Scriptures, we observe a particular kind of form and craft. Chiseled. Carefully wrought. Architecturally tight. Economical. And he said. Let there be. There was. And he saw. Sevenfold, internally integrated, departures from the form just to show us something fresh. "Very good." "And on the seventh day, God rested."

One could learn Hebrew for the sole purpose of observing this kind of art.

I say this in order to appreciate the difference here, in the thirty-five verses of Psalm 104. Exuberance, metaphors flying ("clothed in majesty," "wrapped in light as with a garment," "clouds as chariots," "flames of fire his servants," "the waters fled, took to flight"), images of joy ("wine that gladdens human hearts, oil to make their faces shine"), mastery ("you set a boundary they cannot cross"), nourishing love ("he waters the mountains from his upper chambers; the land is satisfied by the fruit of his work"), license and freedom ("the beasts of the forest prowl, the lions roar for their prey"), innumerability ("the sea, vast and spacious, teeming with creatures beyond number"), the conjunction of raw power and divine joy and pride ("there the ships go to and fro, and Leviathan, which you formed to frolic there"). Observing all this, newfound humility, praise, and a sense of one's place in the good world God has made.

> May the glory of the LORD endure forever,
>   may the LORD rejoice in his works,
> who looks on the earth and it trembles,
>   who touches the mountains and they smoke!
> I will sing to the LORD as long as I live;
>   I will sing praise to my God while I have being.
> May my meditation be pleasing to him,
>   for I rejoice in the LORD. (Ps 104:31–34)

I believe we have earned the right to let God and the psalmist speak to us. Without interruption. Follow the trail they design. Enter into the spirit with which the psalm ends. At home in God and the world he has made. Praise the LORD, my soul. Praise the LORD.

ASCENT AND ALLELUIA

For the sake of completion, I wish to make a brief comment about the final book of the Psalter (Pss 107–150). Each book makes its unique contribution, just as each leg of the journey of our life, whether valley or mountaintop or plain, says something distinctive to us about our individual lives under God. There are five books of Lamentation, five books of Torah, and five books of Psalms.

Psalm 104 is a sort of high-water mark in the Psalms, extolling God the Creator, exuberant, playful, a release back into life, ordered and whole, before the dealings of his hand.

> Bless the LORD, O my soul!
> O LORD my God, thou art very great!
> Thou art clothed with honor and majesty,
>   who coverest thyself with light as with a garment,
> who hast stretched out the heavens like a tent,
>   who hast laid the beams of thy chambers on the waters,
> who makest the clouds thy chariot,
>   who ridest on the wings of the wind,
> who makest the winds thy messengers,
>   fire and flame thy ministers.
>
> Thou didst set the earth on its foundations,
>   so that it should never be shaken.
> Thou didst cover it with the deep as with a garment;
>   the waters stood above the mountains.
> At thy rebuke they fled;
>   at the sound of thy thunder they took to flight.
> The mountains rose, the valleys sank down
>   to the place which thou didst appoint for them.

Thou didst set a bound which they should not pass,
    so that they might not again cover the earth.

Thou makest springs gush forth in the valleys;
    they flow between the hills,
they give drink to every beast of the field;
    the wild asses quench their thirst.
By them the birds of the air have their habitation;
    they sing among the branches.
From thy lofty abode thou waterest the mountains;
    the earth is satisfied with the fruit of thy work.

Thou dost cause the grass to grow for the cattle,
    and plants for man to cultivate,
that he may bring forth food from the earth,
    and wine to gladden the heart of man,
oil to make his face shine,
    and bread to strengthen man's heart.
The trees of the Lord are watered abundantly,
    the cedars of Lebanon which he planted.
In them the birds build their nests;
    the stork has her home in the fir trees.
The high mountains are for the wild goats;
    the rocks are a refuge for the badgers.
Thou hast made the moon to mark the seasons;
    the sun knows its time for setting.
Thou makest darkness, and it is night,
    when all the beasts of the forest creep forth.
The young lions roar for their prey,
    seeking their food from God.
When the sun rises, they get them away
    and lie down in their dens.
Man goes forth to his work
    and to his labor until the evening.

O Lord, how manifold are thy works!
    In wisdom hast thou made them all;
    the earth is full of thy creatures.
Yonder is the sea, great and wide,
    which teems with things innumerable,
    living things both small and great.

There go the ships,
    and Leviathan which thou didst form to sport in it.

These all look to thee,
    to give them their food in due season.
When thou givest to them, they gather it up;
    when thou openest thy hand, they are filled with good
        things.
When thou hidest thy face, they are dismayed;
    when thou takest away their breath, they die
    and return to their dust.
When thou sendest forth thy Spirit, they are created;
    and thou renewest the face of the ground.

May the glory of the LORD endure for ever,
    may the LORD rejoice in his works,
who looks on the earth and it trembles,
    who touches the mountains and they smoke!
I will sing to the LORD as long as I live;
    I will sing praise to my God while I have being.
May my meditation be pleasing to him,
    for I rejoice in the LORD.
Let sinners be consumed from the earth,
    and let the wicked be no more!
Bless the LORD, O my soul!
Praise the LORD! (Ps 104)

In Book Five we see three special features. David has returned! The man of music and prayer. Fourteen of the final forty-four psalms are provided with an ascription bearing his name. God's covenant with David has held. The God of creation has kept his promises. We may take as plausible that the "David" appearing here represents something of the continued hope for the King of Kings, who will come in the fullness of time, Son of David, Son of God.

And this David, quite properly, lives inside the world of Ascent. A word pregnant with meaning and hope. The physical ascent one might well imagine, as exiled Israel returns, climbing the paths to Zion, home again. The spiritual ascent we all are making on the road with God. From valley to heights to his throne in heaven. Where he sits enthroned above the flood, in the fellowship of Son and Holy Spirit, from whence all love and life flow. The life of love shared between them, which broke forth in love, in the creation of all things visible and invisible, and man made in his image and likeness. You and me.

The Psalms of Ascent, fifteen in number, clustered in one block, running from Psalm 120 to Psalm 134. Standing alone, or with the added attribution, "Of David." David and us. Even one with the addition, "Of Solomon." The promises to David and his lineage, and those of us on pilgrimage in life, following the King of Kings.

And praise. The word in Hebrew, "praise to the LORD," or in English, now a familiar word, the simple rendering of the Hebrew itself, pulled into our languages, "Alleluia." I can say there are ten such psalms and you can see them easily enough yourself, in this final section. But that would not capture the essence of their significance, which has less to do with quantity than quality and form.

You do not need to know Hebrew to spot this formal significance. Anyone can see it. You point out the word written in Hebrew script *hallelu-ya* where it appears at the head of Psalm 146, and where it has been heading there in preceding psalms. Once this is grasped, you enter fully into the final sanctuary of the last five psalms, five being the number of totality: five books of praise, instruction, lamentation. They all begin with this command to praise, starting in Psalm 146 and 147. Now you are able to see the special, repeated hallelu-ya, "praise the LORD," in Psalm 148, nine times in close succession, in verses 1–5. Visually distinct. As though the Holy Spirit wants to assist those without Hebrew to see the word all the same.

Now the final psalm can register its glossolalia of "endless praise." A dozen, plus one times.

The theme word is הַלְלוּהוּ.

הַלְלוּ יָהּו הַלְלוּ־אֵל בְּקָדְשׁוֹ הַלְל ּוּהוּ בִּרְקִיע עֻזּוֹ׃
הַלְלוּהוּ בִגְבוּרֹתָיו הַלְל ּוּהוּ כְּרֹב גֻּדְלוֹ׃
הַלְלוּהוּ בְּתֵקַע שׁוֹפָר הַלְל ּוּהוּ בְּנֵבֶל וְכִנּוֹר׃
הַלְלוּהוּ בְתֹף וּמָחוֹל הַלְל ּוּהוּ בְּמִנּים וְעוּגָב׃
הַלְלוּהוּ בְצִלְצְלֵי־שָׁמַע הַלְל ּוּהוּ בְּצִלְצְלֵי תְרוּעָה׃
כֹּל הַנְּשָׁמָה תְּהַלֵּל יָהּ הַלְלוּ־יָהּ׃

You can see it repeated and repeated and repeated, trying to do justice to what must be said. "Let all that has breath praise Him. Praise him." An "ending" that is always and forever stretching out before us.

It belongs to the wisdom and purpose of the Psalter to take us on a journey. We come alongside David, Moses, unknown and anonymous pray-ers, choral experts. We see the beautiful design and architecture of the acrostic poems, each line or stanza with an alphabetic progress, A to Z, at the start of the line. We go into places of doubt and dread. We see the journey of God's people with their LORD. We join them in psalms of praise and thanksgiving.

I suppose one could say that every journey of the written word must come to its conclusion. But the Psalms seem to find a different way. We don't come to an end, but ascend. Every writer struggles to find the way to bring the story to a proper conclusion. The Psalter bids us start again. The Scriptures are not writings about which we say, "I've already read that." They continually press upon us the horizon of God's bounty and purposes, which shifts in proportion to where we find ourselves in life. Our feet swing like the child's, "Do it again, do it again." And God and his Word graciously oblige.

We have been paying special attention to God the Creator, stiller of the seas, preparer of dry land, sending forth winds and clouds at his breath, marveling at innumerability and the vast scale of all things, beyond the capacity of human comprehension, and delighting in all that he has made, bringing him joy in the beholding.

Psalm 104 holds a kind of pride of place in this, its deep purpose seen best when we feel the lights could go out, when the way is darkened, when God's voice seems thinned out to silence, more profound than anything we have known. And then, bursting forth, creation raises its voice to sing his eternal praises, and we are back at home again, chastened, restored, and studying a new horizon of his purposes for us.

As we march up the path of his ascending grace, we get to speak to God. Unable to gather our words to fit the high purpose of praising him, we do the only thing left for us, we who have come to learn of him as the Maker of all things, the Creator of life and beauty, our majestic LORD.

We call on all that he has made to raise their voices in praise, a chorus of endless Alleluia.

> Praise the LORD!
> Praise the LORD from the heavens,
>   praise him in the heights!
> Praise him, all his angels;
>   praise him, all his host!
>
> Praise him, sun and moon,
>   praise him, all you shining stars!
> Praise him, you highest heavens,
>   and you waters above the heavens!
>
> Let them praise the name of the LORD!
>   For he commanded and they were created.
> And he established them for ever and ever;
>   he fixed their bounds which cannot be passed.
>
> Praise the LORD from the earth,
>   you sea monsters and all deeps,
> fire and hail, snow and frost,
>   stormy wind fulfilling his command!
>
> Mountains and all hills,
>   fruit trees and all cedars!

Beasts and all cattle,
   creeping things and flying birds!

Kings of the earth and all peoples,
   princes and all rulers of the earth!
Young men and maidens together,
   old men and children!

Let them praise the name of the LORD,
   for his name alone is exalted;
      his glory is above earth and heaven.
He has raised up a horn for his people,
   praise for all his saints,
      for the people of Israel who are near to him.
Praise the LORD! (Ps 148)

I started this small book with some reminiscences from my days in boarding school in the mountains of western North Carolina. My mind returns to these as we move from the Psalter to the speeches of God the Creator in the book of Job.

When we were victorious on the football field, tennis court, gym, wrestling mat, or cross-country trail, we got to celebrate by singing a special hymn at Evensong, as the day came to a close and we headed off to dinner and study hall.

I can still remember it, even though it is quite obscure, hunkered down in some corner of the 1940 hymnal we used in those days. I can bring to mind its few short and punctuated verses, though I haven't sung it since. This is because it held such a special place in our days there.

And because, for these special occasions of victory, the chaplain (my dad) agreed to give way and let us sing it in as full a volume as we could muster, with song bursting into shouts of joy. Not that he had much choice.

Sing alleluia forth in duteous praise,
   Ye citizens of heaven O sweetly raise
An endless Alleluia!

Ye powers, who stand before the eternal Light,
  In hymning choirs re-echo to the height,
An endless Alleluia.

The holy city shall take up your strain,
  And with glad songs resounding wake again
An endless Alleluia.

There, in one grand acclaim, forever ring
  The strains which tell the honor of your king,
An endless Alleluia.

Almighty Christ, to Thee our voices sing
  Glory forevermore; to Thee we bring
An endless Alleluia.

I can think of no better way to end these reflections. The hymn captures something of the exuberant and full-throated way the Psalter reaches its final crescendo. An endless Alleluia.

PART II
THE WITNESS OF JOB

THE MAJESTY OF THE
CREATOR AND HIS WORLD

I want now to turn to God's address to Job "from the whirlwind," constituting the four climactic chapters (38–41) and setting the stage for his restoration with which the book closes (chap. 42). Where God allows creation to speak for him in his address to Job.

This unusual address baffles or irritates modern readers. In what way does what is said address the dilemma we have been witnessing? Painful, poignant, anguished suffering, infuriating the man Job, in three rounds of back-and-forth where Job's acquaintances seek to comfort him (or so they start), but end up battering him in ways unspeakably cruel. As has been noted, they become something of an extension of the wretched and near-death assaults of Satan visited upon Job in the opening chapters.

The bulk of the book consists of these "dialogues" (the word can serve as a shorthand, though a poor one given what we hear), running from chapter 3 to the entrance of a certain Elihu at chapter 32. Elihu speaks for six chapters in a manner unclear as to purpose or resolution. To the degree that he retards the action and the forward movement of the plot—how will Job's dilemma be resolved?—his long-windedness merely heightens our need to hear from the only person capable of entering the drama and providing a resolution. God. Job has said as much, and we know as much. And speak God finally and majestically does.

Because the inadequacy of the response—given the content, form, and design of what we have been witnessing—is the verdict rendered by many modern commentators and readers, one cannot allow the creation there so depicted to speak to us within the scope of just these four chapters alone. Unless one wants to read between the lines or say Job's own response to what has been said is tongue-in-cheek or just a resigned "I've had enough"—something the text on its own does not say—this complicates matters. The address of God, using the creation to speak of him, and for him, is the pinnacle of the book of Job. These speeches can only be properly interpreted in the light of the preceding thirty-seven-chapter drama.

What we may struggle to understand, Job not only understands but confesses: it has been anything but unclear and has indeed given him a manner and character of understanding unlike anything he has ever seen or known. Before, within, or after what he hears when God speaks to him in his here and now.

Looking at the response a bit more closely, Job says he has had his entire manner of comprehension shoved onto another plane. He had heard of God by the hearing of the ear. He has heard of him—the unparalleled righteous man of prayer—in the form appropriate to that exalted status. In his speeches uttered in the vortex of misunderstanding and cruelty that has been his lot with his "friends," Job will refer to this exalted and unparalleled status, tragically now in forfeit, and so in the manner of something like retrospective yearning (chaps. 29–30). He laments the memory of days now far in the past and unlikely ever to return to him, given the reduction of his condition to the barest of minimum.

"Oh, that I were as in the months of old . . . when the friendship of God was upon my tent" (29:1, 4). It is hard to hear this anguish without filter. The chapter is a long and moving oration, where Job recalls his exemplary righteousness. Our hearts go out to Job, and whatever excesses in speaking we may have observed and sought to forgive of this man beaten down so severely, these his final words cannot fail to move our hearts. He is a man of God's precious holding and care.

He has heard of God by the hearing of the ear in a way no other ear has heard him. This man, the beloved servant of God, upon whom God is prepared to make repose all his trust, as he walks into the furnace of affliction God has told the satanic challenger he will permit, because in this man Job, he has faith. God will trust Job to defeat the Satan who never shows his face to him, who has said to God, "No one will serve God for *hinnam*"—for nothing but God's own sake, for no reason except the maintenance of a relationship when all else has been stripped away. Where all he held dear, where he could have banked his fires until the awful saga turned to good at last, is gone and it is just him and God alone.

In this sense, the friends over time are just ignored by Job, and the things they say simply ricochet off our hero, who knows to whom what he has to say must be addressed. The God who has allowed all this horrendous suffering to fall upon him, the one man whose relationship with him was unassailable, impeccable, rich, and without parallel in all the creation God surveys—this God Job demands to hear from. And he does.

This man Job, for whom we are still awaiting restoration, after God has spoken to him in the manner he has chosen to speak, says simply to him, "Now my eye sees you." Measured against the exalted form of his relationship to God, the form wherein he has heard him by the hearing of the ear, Job has penetrated through to a higher plane of God's presence, person, and life, now shared with him by means of the words addressed to him in these four chapters, which will form the center of our investigation: God and creation in the address to Job.

Stated simply, Job is seeing something in what has been said to him, something extraordinarily transformative. It isn't merely the fact of an answer—God appears, without words—as opposed to the doubts and browbeating of the friends and of Elihu, the exasperated latecomer who purports to be bringing something new to the playing field. His final contribution is the pious and stately, "The Almighty—we cannot find him." No, God arrives. And God speaks.

God strides onto the field of play so forcefully, with a display of authority and overwhelming presence so present and so powerful, as to cause Job to scramble for some bit of solid ground before this unrivaled display of majesty. "I am of small account," he says when he catches his breath. "I lay my hand on my mouth." But this only leads to a second speech to follow the first in equal or mounting—given the accumulation and full weight of what is being said—intensity.

The other small detail in Job's final response, to which we are paying attention here, is the oddity that in speaking of another plane of comprehension and saying this to God directly (we "overhear" it, as it were), Job does something not really necessary. Something unexpected. Twice. He makes his acknowledgment to God, and next to that direct speech to him, he quotes and intersperses God's own words uttered earlier to him. He speaks back to God what God has said to him when he addressed him. "Who is this that hides counsel without knowledge?" and "Hear, and I will speak; I will question you, and you declare to me."

Now, manifestly, Job does not need to remind God of what he has just now said to him, and neither, strictly speaking, does Job need to say this in the context of his direct response to God in his own words—a response sufficient and full of significance, having to do with transformed comprehension.

It is as though this taking upon his lips of God's words spoken to him constitutes a kind of one-to-one exchange, a form of communication between God and Job in which an equivalence is being established, in the most minimal and modest form possible between God Almighty and man made in his image. Job takes God's speech to him and lodges it inside his response to God, where a higher plane of comprehension is being reported and acknowledged. From Job to God. And, in a measure of speaking, from God to Job, now held within Job's own breast.

The Freedom of
Job and of God

From what has been said thus far, it should be clear that unpersuasive is the view that the response to Job by God is quirky, something pasted in by inadequate editors, insulting in its transcendence and its tone, a piece of irrelevance in a book about innocent suffering and its causes. "When you're blue, go to the zoo," as a former teacher put it.

The book of Job is not about why innocent people suffer. No book can be written to explain that. Why people suffer is the consequence of the fragile world in which we live and the aftershocks of an evil that God has put in the dock, defeated by the cross of his Son, upon whom every grief we know has been visited and borne in love, but which lashes the world, until he comes in glory.

No, the book of Job is about a Singular Saint. Not an Everyman of Common Suffering. God's hugely adored friend, and deservedly so, who arises every morning to pray lest his sons sinned by omission or commission.

It is critical to respect the horizon on which he finds his path. He is not an Israelite. This belongs to his specificity and particularity. In the mind of the author—like Shakespeare faithfully rendering an age not his own—he belongs to the world of creation. He precedes the covenants with the people of God's special choosing. His contemporary is Noah (see Ezek 14). He lives in the world prior to God's creating and electing of Israel, in that place where rare, exemplary heroes arise to warm God's heart. "Have you seen anyone like my servant Job?" God proudly asks.

He wears his own "cloak of many colors," more resplendent by a factor incalculable than the boy Joseph. Appropriate to the time of God and Job. He is a man of the East, mysterious in anonymity. A man who comes before God's ordering of the world in his calling of Abraham, and the beginning of "history"—a history of what it means for God to create and call and inhabit life with a people. A story requires someone to record it—the origins of what we call inspiration. A gifted place in time to observe time.

So, in this sense he is no Everyman who suffers, but a Special Man, as a theologian with a heart has put it, a "type of Jesus Christ." As Jesus is particular, as his relationship with God is particular, so is the man Job, within the age of God's disposing, close to the dawn of creation. In the counsel of his own divine fellowship, God announces his love and trust, invested in this one man, Job.

To properly understand this book, we have to consider the freedom of God and the freedom of Job. The freely disposed affection and trust that God places in his freely chosen man, soon to embark on a hard journey. The freely chosen affection, trust, and righteousness that Job has disposed in the God who is his true home, above all things. Where he is who he is, where he knows whither he goes, under whose wings is everything that constitutes his life and his future. This is the Job of the book before us, asking to be read and followed according to this rule and way. Only in this way can we understand what God says to Job when he, at last, speaks.

Job exists in the freedom of God's affection and pride, and God says that he agrees with everything about the disposition, he to Job and Job to him. It constitutes the place of full agreement around which everything we read unfolds. We have to have this special place always before our eyes if we are to plot the path that will unfold and understand the way God speaks to his Special Man when speak he does. To understand the character of the ordeal that we watch Job endure.

The loss of children, goods, possessions—the tragic stripping, *la décapage*, of the man from Uz—is never the subject of the laments of Job in the central portion of the book. Now this is striking and worthy of consideration.

The absence of reference to them cannot be brushed to the side on the basis of a theory of the book's theoretical coming-to-be. As the diachronic account goes: there was once a folktale about a patient Job, consisting of opening and concluding sections (the "Frame Narrative") that the Dialogue section was added to without any reference to or need of coordination—the entry hall opening the reader into the vestibule and main rooms of the house where Job's ordeal unfolds. So, failure to mention the horrible dispossession is the consequence of the Dialogues and Frame Narrative having distinctive and independent histories before being conjoined in the present book.

Yet we have already seen how, at the conclusion of this same main Dialogue section (see 29–30), Job does mourn the loss of his exalted status and special life with God. This is not a sustained theme in what precedes. The friends' hounding and abuse of Job explains in part how his complaints turn in another direction.

They are the ones who make this about God and the guilt of Job. They corral the matter and force it into this narrow mold. Again and again, they press Job to confess his misdeeds and the things that alone could account for his pitiful condition *coram deo*. And this he resolutely refuses to do. Without for a second entertaining their mechanical and bloodless "theology"—turning God into a sort of faceless theory, draining him of life and love—Job betters them on the same field of play. *His dilemma is indeed about God.* The God whose relationship to him was the rudder, sail, and ship of his life. The source of his identity, purpose, and life.

Let us hear Job speak. His final words before his solemn demand that God appear and speak to him.

> "Oh, that I were as in the months of old,
>   as in the days when God watched over me;
> when his lamp shone upon my head,
>   and by his light I walked through darkness;

as I was in my autumn days,
  when the friendship of God was upon my tent;
when the Almighty was yet with me,
  when my children were about me;
when my steps were washed with milk,
  and the rock poured out for me streams of oil!
When I went to the gate of the city,
  when I prepared my seat in the square,
the young men saw me and withdrew,
  and the aged rose and stood;
the princes refrained from talking,
  and laid their hand on their mouth;
the voice of the nobles was hushed,
  and their tongues cleaved to the roof of their mouth.
When the ear heard, it called me blessed,
  and when the eye saw, it approved;
because I delivered the poor who cried,
  and the fatherless who had none to help him.
The blessing of him who was about to perish came upon me,
  and I caused the widow's heart to sing for joy.
I put on righteousness, and it clothed me;
  my justice was like a robe and a turban.
I was eyes to the blind,
  and feet to the lame.
I was a father to the poor,
  and I searched out the cause of him whom I did not know.
I broke the fangs of the unrighteous,
  and made him drop his prey from his teeth.
Then I thought, 'I shall die in my nest,
  and I shall multiply my days as the sand,
my roots spread out to the waters,
  with the dew all night on my branches,
my glory fresh with me,
  and my bow ever new in my hand.'

"Men listened to me, and waited,
  and kept silence for my counsel.
After I spoke they did not speak again,
  and my word dropped upon them.

They waited for me as for the rain;
   they opened their mouths as for the spring rain.
I smiled on them when they had no confidence;
   the light of my countenance they did not cast down.
I chose their way, and sat as chief,
   and I dwelt like a king among his troops,
   like one who comforts mourners." (29:2–25)

In the opening chapters, we are told of Job's matchless status, from the mouth of God himself. And the narrator lets us see concrete examples of it. But here, it is Job speaking for himself. This "adamantine certainty" (Barth, CD IV.3.1, 386) of his cause and of his righteousness would be considered blasphemous on the lips of an Everyman. Here we see the Dialogues and Frame Narrative in agreement, God and Job and the omniscient narrator rendering the same verdict from three directions. Having silenced the friends and outdistanced the terrain on which their repetitive and one-dimensional arguments functioned, Job breaks free and tells us proudly who he is. From the pitiable wreck of his present existence, he musters strength and pulls from the wardrobe of his past the robe and turban of his rich life with God.

It is on this basis, and the ordeal he has endured to the end, standing now alone before God, that he makes his final appeal and demand that God appear and speak.

GOD ANSWERS JOB
Tone and Form

The only way, I believe, we can understand the manner in which God responds to Job is to keep firmly in view the Job we are talking about. This is the unparalleled man of righteousness. The one in whom God has placed his trust. Whom he has allowed to be reduced to the barest of minimum. The Job God trusts. The Job in whom the wager with the powers of darkness—you only have faithful followers because you do good things for them; you have put a hedge about them—is allowed to be played out.

We have just heard Job sum up the life he had once with God. It is not a report card that Everyman produces. It is a life lived under and before God about which God in the heavenly council had reason to boast and call upon the full light of heaven to attest to.

In his final speeches—the friends mercifully put off the field of play, their exchanges fizzling out in round three—Job rises up in his full strength and self-prepossession. His adamantine confidence has proved more than a match for the assaults thrown at him, all the more remarkable after such a reduction of his life and such a merciless browbeating at the hands of his "friends." They have run out of gas. Job's tank is remarkably full.

Let us call it what it is. He is about the business of defeating not just the associates observing his life on the ash-heap, but also the unknown force of darkness—the source of disease, assault, and death—with which he is contending, against which the trust of God has been deposited in a wager proving to be a good one, in the hands of this noble hero. He has risen up and endured to the end. The singularity of his situation has as the only parallel that of Jesus Christ. Job is no Christ. But he is a type of Christ. Job and Christ freely entrusted with the honor of God himself, freely experiencing trials and the assaults of the devil so as to defeat him and honor God.

The English word "patience" has suffered the fate of many words and can be instinctively associated with silent resignation and waiting—the polar opposite of what we see in Job. The word appearing in the Epistle of James, in Greek *upomone*, means literally to remain standing after others have fled. To stand under. To persevere. To stand fast. The adjective steadfast, stayed-fast, is just what this means.

Here is the Job whom God does indeed address—in spite of the cosmic handwaving and portentous obfuscations of the young Elihu, droning on at length, as both we and Job wait for God to appear. Where else could this drama go? God must appear.

And he does. Here it is important to keep in mind that what we are viewing and hearing we are "overhearing." God is not speaking to us, except by bank shot. It is fair to say that we too are being tested as we observe this ordeal. But our test is our own, however much suffering and anguish come our way, and come they do. We may learn from Job, but only by allowing Job to be Job, the man in whom God has utmost pride and trust. In the context of his personal address to Job, God is speaking to this man, inside of this unique and particular drama.

Another way to say this is, we know why Job is suffering. Job does not. He can only defeat the force of darkness at the center of his cruel ordeal if he never knows why he has been asked to tread this path. Otherwise, his faithfulness to God would not be "for nought" but would devolve instead into a scheme or stratagem independent of the Living God whose trust has been deposited upon him.

So, why does God appear as he does and speak as he does? We have noted that, on his side, he too does not provide answers that the reader might be looking for. He neither consoles nor explains. This is consistent with what Job says when God has at last finished what he has chosen to say to him. He does not say, "Thanks for the explanation"—not simply because God doesn't give one, but because it does not sound like what Job was looking for either.

Job has railed against God—to the point of excess, one might argue. He has said repeatedly that God has become alien to him and that the odd form in which he now appears to him is in fact too proximate. He wants God to leave him alone but demands that he take a position alike unto how he once knew him. He refuses to accept that God is coming to him in this form. His complaint is not about the lack of an answer to suffering. His complaint is that God is unrecognizable to him and that he must cease that and be again the God of his giving, and not the God of his taking away. A pious sentiment offered by Job after the first attack from Satan that he endures, that he then must swallow to the dregs on the path down which he will go.

The fact that the friends insist on being theologians, arguing that God is like this or that, of course forces the course of the dialogues and the terrain on which Job does his processing of his condition and the character of God coming now at him.

In short, the "answer" that Job is looking for, the resolution he is seeking, entails God himself. He demands an encounter. He will see the God who has become alien to him. Not ideas, consolation, explanation, but God. The friends say, the problem here is you. Job says, no, it is God. He is more right in what he says than the friends, but also, in the anguish in which he finds himself, likely unprepared for the alien God to show himself in the manner that he is about to.

It is the disjunction between who he once was and who he has become, who God once was and now is—it is this gap that Job demands be closed. It is a titanic struggle in his soul. We have walked along with him and have seen how boxed in he is, and so we also, if we listen to Job closely, must want what he wants. God.

We are, however, only witnesses of this titanic struggle; we are not experiencing it on the terms that Job is. It is his massive disjunction, not ours, and so we must let God close the gap for Job on the terms he alone knows.

The series of questions God poses to his unparalleled friend and trust-bearer begins with a direct appeal to Job. In the form of a command to him. Out of the whirlwind, wherein his alien form resides, he addresses Job and tells him to prepare himself. We immediately get the drift that God means to be God. For that to be so, he will ask questions that Job is unable, in the nature of the case, to answer. He has darkened the situation given the dark trail on which he has found himself. Now God tells him to gird up his loins.

Barth handles this dimension well when he says,

> The primary subject of his complaints, consists in the conjunction of his profound knowledge that in what has happened and what has come on him he has to do with God, and his no less profound ignorance how far he has to do with God. (*CD* IV.3.1, 401)

So now God will close the gap on his side.

Yet the questions he will begin to unroll—first about the created order in its primordial form, and then about the creatures whose ways are strange and untamed to man's eye and mind—are not just meant to shut Job up or to overwhelm and crush him. God knows what his servant has been and is enduring. That is not his intention. Job is up to what he is going to show him, as much as he is going to show him.

By posing these questions, questions only God can pose and only God can answer, Job's request is being met. Is so doing, furthermore, God is disclosing something to him he has never disclosed to anyone. The questions he cannot answer also show Job who God is, as Creator and as God. They intimate him and show that we can always only ever see the outskirts of God, and that Job is seeing more than any of us ever will. This will prove to be enough, as Job responds in the end. His eye has seen God.

Job is a type of Christ, walking the unique trail of trust-bearing that is his to walk, in the providence of God, not as weighty and not as salvific, but towering over the Everyman of our common experience in life. A guide, a mentor, when we must also walk into darkness.

THE MAJESTY OF CREATION
IN JOB AND IN THE PSALMS

My purpose in examining the majesty of God in the Psalms speaks for itself. I have taken that journey with the psalmist to try to understand the role of God as Creator and its place within the inspired reflections on this topic in sacred scripture.

In a way I have wanted to explore, it also can potentially help us understand the form and content of what God says to Job in the four chapters of his speaking. The points of contact between Job 38–41 and the Psalms are obvious enough and at certain places we can sense a direct association: the foundations of the earth, the holding back of the flood waters at creation and in the exertion of daily authority over chaos such as we see in the Psalms, the creational and meteorological similarities, and so forth. There are also some obvious parallels with verses in chapter 40 of Isaiah.

> Who has measured the waters in the hollow of his hand
> and marked off the heavens with a span,
> enclosed the dust of the earth in a measure
> and weighed the mountains in scales
> and the hills in a balance? (Isa 40:12)

We have the same question-form appearing in Isaiah and in Job. The Psalms usually don't operate along this axis. They represent inspired declarations about God and creation, as the psalmist is given to lift his eyes to the created order, note what he sees, and praise God for his "creation, preservation, and all the blessings of this life" (as the General Thanksgiving used in Morning Prayer summarizes it).

In Isaiah 40, the prophet is speaking from the heavenly council. We see things from his eye, who is gifted to see things as God sees them.

Here in Job, the form (praise of God the Creator) and its subtle variations give way to a different manner of declaration. God is speaking without any assistance. He is inspiring no one, and he is not asking the eye of the prophet to speak for him. Job has asked for him, demanded that he appear. He is obliging.

For Job to see God, he must be given a vision of things that only pertain to God and his majesty. God being God, as it were. Not God condescending to inspire the psalmist or bestow his word by means of prophetic endowment. Not God condescending to speak on terms appropriate to hearing him, frail and limited as we are, but God taking Job up into his world, as it were. You asked for me. Here I am. My God's-eye view. For that, you must gird up your loins. Incomparable servant, invested with my trust, let's walk out onto the terrain of divine incomparability.

I have become alien to you, Job. There is a reason why that is so. In respect to human life and its ways, even the exalted and the utterly wretched ways I have asked you, Job, to tread. In the end, I am alien. But let me show you just what that looks like. Let me close the gap, the unbearable disjuncture torturing you, and the distance between me as alien and me as your treasured God of erstwhile service, let me bring you onto a plane appropriate for what I have asked of you, and for the trust I have deposited on your soul. You will need to brace yourself.

I am posing questions you cannot answer in order to show you who I am and in order to un-darken the counsel of your limited knowledge (38:1). I am going to change that. In the end, though you cannot answer now, you will indeed declare to me.

Barth refers to this as God's wager all over again. His trust that, in what he will show Job, in meeting Job's demand to appear on the terms appropriate to being God, he is taking a risk. The quote is worth citing in detail as it will help us to understand how

God talks as he does, given that he wants Job to answer him when he is done.

> He answers Job's appeal to him by making an appeal of His own to Job. The Word spoken to him does not merely come to him, or pass over him and away like a monstrous roller. It comes right into him. Indeed, it is to be uttered by himself as his own word [see above on Job quoting God in his response], as the confession of his own heart and lips. God allows everything to depend on this recognition and confession. What a risk! Job might do no more than gape at the book of nature unfolded before him. He might perhaps find aesthetic enjoyment in some of the forms, and be shocked by others. He might simply close his eyes in disgust. He might make nothing of it all or misunderstand it. He might make no answer at all, or only the answer of silence, to the question put to him. God would then have wasted His time with him. He would have beaten the air. The lesson would have failed. No decision would have been reached. For it was essential to such a decision that Job himself should answer, and answer correctly. Otherwise, he would have resumed his old complaint and accusation, and could have continued it *ad infinitum*. Indeed, he would have had to do so. At the end of the Book God Himself would then have been the true and great loser. But so great is the sovereignty of the Teacher who undertakes this instruction that He does not fear this risk. So free is God that He dares to have dealings with the free man Job. We might almost say that He again wagers on Job and wins again as Job's answer shows. (Barth, *CD* IV.3.1, 430–31)

It is useful to have this wider perspective as we seek to understand and come to terms with what God says to Job and why he speaks as he does, opening the book of creation in the manner that he does.

And I believe I am now at a place where the question of the content of the divine speeches, and their place in the book of Job, can best be answered. In this we are assisted by the Psalter and its presentation of God as Creator.

The matter can be stated thus. It isn't a matter of asking why God speaks as he does. It is, rather, the recognition and acknowledgment that *he must speak as he does*. He must speak from the terrain known only to him. He must speak as only God can speak, and in no other way. This is what Job has demanded. Only in this way can the familiar God, longed for by Job and demanded by him in his ordeal, and the alien God show themselves to be one and the same God. To ask about the content of the speeches as if they were something detachable and open for evaluation, and not the necessary speech that establishes God as God in the world of Job's suffering, is to misunderstand why God is using creation as the plane on which he must speak to Job. Only here can the gap between notions of "the familiar" and "the alien" be closed. God isn't alien and he isn't familiar. He is God, and his transcendence and his presentation to Job of his creation are intended truly to address Job in the dilemma facing him. A real dilemma. One that God understands. The very road on which he has himself placed Job, as the beloved man from Uz, is responsible for the terrible disjunction rising up within that man, tearing him apart and leaving him at a place where only God can meet him. And so he does.

THE DIVINE RESPONSE

The direction of travel set by this book is to look at what God has to say to Job, given the way the majesty of God functions in the Psalms, so as to evaluate the distinctiveness of the book of Job's contribution to this theme. We are ready to do that, having set the proper context for God's singular address to the singular man Job.

The presentation of chapters 38–41 is soaring and far more ambitious, if that is the correct word, than what the Psalms display—and that is a tall order. The reason for this is the perspective of the divine speeches. We have not the inspired psalmist's angle of vision, soaring in its own register (see Ps 104), but rather a God's-eye view. This belongs to the logic of the book of Job and it follows on from the demand of Job that God appear.

We can examine the response—some 120 verses in length; that is itself unique vis-à-vis the Psalms—according to the distinct topics being set forth for Job's beholding. The response uses for the most part a question form. Can you? Do you? But not exclusively. In chapter 39, for example, the form is broken so that sections of detailed description can be accommodated (39:13–18, 21–25, 28–30). The presentation of Behemoth functions likewise (40:15–24). And after questioning Job about his ability to tangle with Leviathan, God lavishly details the sea monster's attributes for twenty-three verses, which constitute his final words to Job (41:12–34).

I note this alternation in form because I'd like to modify the question-form in the opening address. I am not doing this to "soften" the address to Job, but rather to try and capture the force of what God is saying. I want to bring the address here more into line with the presentation of the majesty of God in creation such as we have examined it in the Psalter. I have spoken at length in the sections above about the uniqueness of Job and of God such as we find it in this ambitious portrayal and dramatic unfolding, constituting the book of Job before us. I am not seeking to undo that.

I believe this rendering more closely aligns with the address God is making. We already know that God is God and Job is man. The question-form certainly drives that point home with absolute force. But it also tilts in the direction of appearing to overwhelm or even shut Job down, which is manifestly not what God is seeking to do when at last he appears and speaks. Sufficient has been said on this point in the previous section. God is seeking a response. He is not seeking to bluster and silence this man in whom he has invested his trust, that Job will prove to be up to defeating the dark forces that have been unleashed upon him. In listening and in what he will respond, he is indeed serving God "for nought." More on the actual denouement of the plot below.

I begin, then, with the first main section of the 120-verse response: God as Creator of the cosmos. I leave the question-form alone at points. Translations of words and intentions are an imprecise business. I believe I am capturing the actual purpose and intention of God's address in the form that ensues.

Section 1 (38:1–38):

> Then the LORD answered Job out of the whirlwind:
>
> "Who is this that darkens counsel by words without
>   knowledge?
> Gird up your loins like a man,
>   I will tell you who I am, and you shall declare to me.
>
> "It is I who laid the foundation of the earth; this is who I am.
> I determined its measurements—now you hear this from
>   my own mouth;
> I stretched the line upon it.
>
> "I determined on what its bases would be sunk,
>   and laid its cornerstone,

when the morning stars sang together,
    and all the sons of God shouted for joy.

"My hand shut in the sea with doors,
    when it burst forth from the womb;
I made clouds a garment for the sea,
    and thick darkness its swaddling band,
I prescribed bounds for it,
    and set bars and doors,
and said, 'Thus far shall you come, and no farther,
    and here shall your proud waves be stayed.'

"I commanded the morning since your days began,
    and caused the dawn to know its place,
that it might take hold of the skirts of the earth,
    and the wicked be shaken out of it.
It is changed like clay under the seal,
    and it is dyed like a garment.
From the wicked their light is withheld,
    and their uplifted arm is broken.
Have you entered into the springs of the sea,
    or walked in the recesses of the deep? No.
I am in charge of the gates of death,
    as well as the gates of deep darkness.
You cannot comprehend the expanse of the earth.
    Only I am able to declare this.
I know the way to the dwelling of light,
    and the location of the place of darkness,
I alone can take you to its territory
    and show you how to discern the paths to its home
To know this, you would have had to be born then,
    and the number of your days as great as my own!

"Have you entered the storehouses of the snow,
    or have you seen the storehouses of the hail,
which I have reserved for the time of trouble,
    for the day of battle and war?
The way to the place where the light is distributed,
    or where the east wind is scattered upon the earth—
I alone know this.

"I cleft a channel for the torrents of rain,
    and a way for the thunderbolt,

to bring rain on a land where no man is,
    on the desert in which there is no man;
to satisfy the waste and desolate land,
    and to make the ground put forth grass.
Has the rain a father,
    or who has begotten the drops of dew?
From whose womb did the ice come forth,
    and who has given birth to the hoarfrost of heaven?
The waters become hard like stone,
    and the face of the deep is frozen.

"You are not able to bind the chains of the Plei'ades,
    or loose the cords of Orion, for that is my domain.
Can you lead forth the Maz'zaroth in their season,
    or can you guide the Bear with its children?
Do you know the ordinances of the heavens?
    Can you establish their rule on the earth?
Can you lift up your voice to the clouds,
    that a flood of waters may cover you?
Can you send forth lightnings, that they may go
    and say to you, 'Here we are'?
I, the LORD, have charge of these.
I put wisdom in the clouds,
    and gave understanding to the mists.
No one can number the clouds by wisdom
    or tilt the waterskins of the heavens,
when the dust runs into a mass
    and the clods cleave fast together.

"I am the LORD you have called upon.
    I am here before you. I am speaking to you. God to Job.
        I-Thou."

It is possible to note similarities between the Psalms extolling the created order and lines from what we read here. The stock and trade of certain historical-critical (and form-critical) investigation would wish to plot the distinctives and create a grid of development and social location. That is not my purpose, as I am seeking to understand the speeches as integral and as indispensable to the way the book of Job says what it wishes to say.

What is of greater interest to this study is the character of this 120-verse response and its unique form within the world of Job's impasse and resolution (it is hoped). The God's-eye view it adopts and the necessary conditions of it establishing the answer to Job, who has demanded to see God, are paramount here. God says Job's counsel is darkened—his painful dilemma in which God is alien and not as he once was, has created this darkness—and that he is lacking true knowledge of the state of affairs. On these matters solely, one suspects Job would agree, and one would also nurse the expectation that Job too will come to agree as we march along with him.

Having set these terms, God speaks. The question-form clearly is intended to show us both that Job has no answer to give and also that he might well interrupt the rat-a-tat volley coming at him. But that does not happen.

The first thing God sets before Job are the primary acts of creation. The mysteries inherent in that cosmic project to which he can only make reference. Creation—seen from the standpoint of the details of God's work—are matters known only to him. We see the results—earth and sea and sky as controlled and not as raw, inchoate matter needing more work—but only God is in a position to open the vault of his deliberations and skills.

One important thing to note is the fairly steady reference to God's capacity to rein things in, to make and also to control and constrain, alongside the notes of mystery—going into the storehouses of snow and hail, or the place where light is distributed, and so forth. God "sits enthroned above the flood" in the lexicon of the Psalms. He is a bulwark against forces of chaos that he has subdued in order to give us an ordered and safe existence.

But there is one thing that lies outside all the vast power and authority and constraint, that lies at the heart of the book before us. He cannot constrain or compel the faithfulness and steadfast relationship Job has with him, and he with Job. The "for nought" hanging over the entire drama belongs in the category of freedom. The free Job and the free God.

Job cannot bind the chains of the Plei'ades as God can. He cannot enter into secret warehouses and zones known only to God. He cannot send forth lightnings or lift his voice to make water come forth from clouds. And God cannot enter into the storehouse of Job's heart and compel him to serve him and remain his loyal friend. He can lift his voice to Job, and he is so doing. But Job will have to lift his own voice and assent to the book of creation being placed before him at the behest of the God he has demanded to speak to him.

Zoological Wonder

Professor Marvin Pope was given the Job commentary assignment in the fledgling (at the time) Anchor Bible series. He was also my Northwest Semitics professor at Yale. There was not as yet a formal grammar for this linguistic field, as the Ugaritic corpus was only unearthed in the early twentieth century. It is an alphabetic language. And a relief in that regard from the syllabary texts of Akkadian—East Semitic—which gave us PhD students nightmares, sleeping between each challenging classroom session, in the form of people speaking unintelligibly in syllabary conversations in our dreams.

Ugaritic, on the other hand, though alphabetic, comes without vowels. Pope handed out some massive grammar in xeroxed and unpublished form and gave us a weekend to read it, and then we started into the bizarre corpus from the ancient Tel called Ras Shamra. We would kid that, without vowels, one could produce relatively interesting translations reading left to right, or right to left. He did not know how to teach; not a criticism. He just could not understand what it meant to be a beginner. A hand would go up and a tentative question posed. In response, he would just put Arabic on the blackboard and say with a smile, "See?"

Upon reflection, it occurs to me that he was producing a sort of minor-league version of what we see in the response of God to Job, in the form and content of the divine speeches of Job he was writing commentary on. Pope saying to us without knowledge, and God saying to Job, "See?"

It was Pope who said of these same exalted speeches—I don't recall where; I don't think he gave himself free rein to say it in print—that they amount to God saying, "When you're blue, go to the zoo." This would be consistent with his wry southern manner, raised no doubt in the usual conservative backwater that bright kids leave to become "biblical scholars."

I have indulged myself here a bit, and I believe Marvin would forgive me (he was later my Yale colleague). He did not take himself too seriously. The Bible for him was a playground for inventive translations (in this he was bested only by Mitchell Dahood, who produced an Anchor Bible translation of the Psalms that no eye has seen before, or since).

"When you're blue, go to the Zoo" rhymes and is a good quip.

Yet, reading this particular segment of God's response to Job (38:39–39:30) shows that, while funny in its way, it is completely wide of the mark. There are no bars on the cages of the animals God shows Job, and that is the point. God has made all the animals, as Genesis summarily tells us, and he will bring them to us, to Job, to man, to see what we shall name them. And whatever name we give them, that will be their name.

There is a lot going on in that cursory statement, but for our purposes, in the context of Job, the animals being shown by God to Job are actually selectively notable. We may have been given the role as stewards to name every single animal God has made, but God has his eye here on a selection, suitable to his particular purposes with the particular man he is addressing.

In the catalog he will present to Job, out of all he could choose to present, we have in order a sevenfold plus one series: lion, raven, mountain goat, wild ass, wild ox, ostrich, horse, hawk. This is an intriguing combination of fearsome might or raw strength (lion and horse, "who laughs at fear") and the marginal (raven), untamed (goat, ass, ox, hawk), or inexplicable (the ostrich who "deals cruelly with her young . . . because God has made her forget wisdom").

Now the fact that God has a choice—out of the vast array of zoological accomplishments in his CV—and that he presents this particular catalog, must deserve our careful attention. In the context of God speaking to Job, in the singular situation the book sets before us, why would these be the examples, out of the myriad he could have recourse to, to set before Job?

The one thing most obvious is that all these creatures are untamable. The use of horses in battle comes in the Persian period, and it represented quite a feat and doubtless instilled terror in the enemy. To get on the back of this animal is something we consider far from unusual, but nothing could be further from the truth. Those who have experienced the thrill of a full gallop know it is akin to riding the wind, only one hoof touching the ground as the horse becomes everything God has made it to be. "He swallows the ground" is God's proud description.

There was a famous scientist at St. Andrews, where I lived and taught for a decade, whose lifetime vocation was to study birdsongs and try to understand why birds sing. You can imagine the obvious theories he spent his years studying with diligence and skill. In the end his verdict, stated not unhappily, was, "I don't know." Something of this same spirit inhabits the world of the selection of animals God displays before Job. Undomesticated and mysterious. Whose patterns are obscure or even senseless to us. The strangely figured and appareled ostrich, cruel to her children, "laughing at the horse and his rider."

I have a French pointing dog whose instincts for spotting game defy any explanation. You don't train them into a dog. God put them there. I have trained dogs, and this dog, whose skills in the field are remarkable—he was number two in French field trials for his breed—I paid to have trained so as to harness his best field potential. He remains stubborn. I like to kid, "disobedient in two languages."

But in reality, he knows what words I am saying to him, and when it is time for business, he responds to my commands. God brought the animals to man to name them. We know the words "raven," "ostrich," "wild ass," and the denominations to which they belong. But unlike my dog, they lie at the outskirts of our world and our words as addressed to them. God is showing Job animals who fly and roam and run and live in realms outside our "home" in life. "The steppe is his home." "Will he spend the night at your crib?" No, he won't.

Only God understands them and what they are up to. He made them, as he made us (on this, see the next chapter). Our wisdom is not up to comprehending them. That is built into the system. The system God has given for them, not for fathoming and control by us. "Why do the songbirds sing?" "I don't know." There is magic and freedom in that admission. Why is Job suffering? It will remain beyond his comprehension. But if God is the one saying that this too is a part of what it means to have Job call for him, and him to answer, then this will be how he points to a reality deeper than suffering and higher than any limitation we feel in our lives. That is what is going to bring Job the peace that allows him to pray again, now even for his three torturing associates, Eliphaz, Bildad, and Zophar.

Job, Behemoth, and Leviathan
God's Final Address

After the zoological response, God turns and addresses Job personally. Job has said nothing thus far and he will speak but briefly here. He confesses that he is awed at what he is being shown, and who is showing it, to the point of silence. "Behold, I am of small account; what shall I answer thee? I lay my hand on my mouth."

He says this in response, presumably, to all he has seen, but also to the direct question God puts to him following what he has thus far said. God addresses the Job who has been accusing him, an obvious reference to his words in the central dialogue section. Cornered by the friends and their accounts of God and what they hold to be Job's guilt responsible for his abject situation, as they see it, Job has taken up his cause directly with the God who has turned alien to him. What God now makes clear is his "faultfinding" with God.

The context for this seems also referred to in Job's response, "I have spoken once, and I will not answer; twice but will proceed no further." Since he hasn't spoken to God in the address to him, until now, by "once, twice" Job is referring to his fulsome speaking in the main section of the book, in the dialogue section with the associates come to condole with him (3–25), and in the series of speeches that follow and end with his demand that God appear (26–31).

But God is not interested in driving Job into silence. He repeats the same words with which he began the first discourse: "Gird up your loins like a man; I will question you and you declare to me." No, God will continue and expect a further declaration from Job.

Yet this time he adds a commentary. This is the first time he has "lowered his visor" (Barth, *CD* IV.3.1, 426). So, what he says is important. "Will you put me in the wrong? Will you condemn me that you may be justified?" He could add, "Why are these the categories you have decided to work with?" Now in the end, God will declare Job right and the friends wrong. It would be too simplistic to think he is referring not to what Job said over against the threesome, but only the noble declaration he makes after the divine speeches, which we will be discussing shortly. The point is that Job is on the right track with God; the friends never are. They wind down and go away. Their fate is not, however, over. We shall see them shortly.

Job has declared God wrong in the sense that, in the form he is coming to him, Job refuses to accept him. He insists that God cannot be as he is. He "justifies himself" in the sense that he declares God must be the familiar God he once knew. These are the compressed two categories he insists circumscribe his life as such and his life with God most especially. With sympathy, one must accept that, because God was the sole radiating point of his whole bearing, the loss of that is insufferable. He was moved to say, after the loss of everything dear to him, "the LORD gives, the LORD takes away" without any hint that he is bartering with God. After he is personally smitten and reduced to the barest of minimum, and after his friends fail to come to him, on his side and on the side of God for him, he inhabits a tortured place where a way forward other than accusation or demand for God to be as once he was to Job cannot be found.

This is the Job before us now.

This is why God "lowers his visor" ever so minimally and says, "I will continue to speak and we shall enter into a place where those two alternatives give way to something grander, something more beautiful, and something finally that will restore peace to your soul. And mine, if I be honest." God wants this, for Job, and for the relationship he insists will be the consequence of Job's holding on and viewing what he has to show him.

God continues on this tack by offering the God-realities to Job. In the realms of justice and the ordering of the broken and sinful world we inhabit, would the exemplary righteous man like to reinhabit the world of his familiar God and handle the domains of conduct alien to God and his ultimate justice and righteousness? If we are moving within the space of these two alternatives, and only them, God says to Job, fine. No one would be better at this than you. The assumed demurral testifies to the point and to Job's silence.

The animals God has just shown Job at the end of his first discourse can be found in the basic zoological textbooks. Now he has something else up his sleeve. What is a Behemoth and what is a Leviathan? Melville answered in *Moby Dick*, and one supposes that the whale he designed—massive in scale and also in metaphysical significance—approached the outskirts of what God shows Job here. Monster crocodiles? Primordial realities whose zoological derivatives we can only guess at?

In our imagination, we can hunt around for dangerous land animals of similar ferocity. Cape buffalo. Rhino. Hippo, my annotation wonders aloud. But surely the point is that these two beasts just aren't in the same zoological textbook as the wild ox or soaring hawk or speeding horse. With them, it isn't a matter of mysterious conduct and maximal free-ranging. It is their sheer ferocity and unparalleled danger, the proximity to which strikes immediate fear and whose proximity to God is what makes them worthy of this present appearance to Job.

God starts with the ostensibly milder of the two monsters. He is a model of taut strength and spring. He fears nothing. No known predators. He roams around in the knowledge and confidence of this, eating as he wishes, never fearing being eaten like every other created creature. This gives him a sort of divine status. Created first. Primordial. No sword of man can be brought near. He views challenges with amusement and insouciance. Raw power need not look in the mirror.

God says he made this beast as he made Job, and this has caused some to think God shows Job the Behemoth in order to hold up a mirror to him. Your conduct is like this beast. Put me among those who think the text would tell us this if it wished, far more directly. Job isn't being put on the analyst's couch. God has better and bigger things in view for the man of his heart. The land monster is the land monster. God has him under his control. The free Job is the free Job.

When we move to God's final address concerning the Leviathan, we ought to sense something of the same energy, confidence, and verve, here on God's side, as what Job delivered on his side in the final address and the appeal he made to God. God's presentation of Leviathan, sustained and uninterrupted, requires little commentary. God is wrapping things up with a crescendo. This is his very best effort. His final word to Job. The details of the sea beast, testimony to his intricate creational pride. The fearsome nature of this beast, meant to place man in man's domain as proper to him, and the sea beast's proper to him.

And this is life. The final divine speech here comes fully alongside the Psalter's own special presentation. God's majestic creation, full of potential danger, a disorder that would threaten our lives, and the inspired deliverances of the psalmist assuring us again and again. Here God is God. His majesty in creation testifies to a realm of beauty, authority, and mercy, of "kingdom, power, and glory," capable of empowerment and transformation, able to turn the darkness of chaos into the brilliant light of his love. This is God speaking to Job. Tell me the most terrifying thing you can. I show you my Leviathan, which I made for the sport of it. All is in my capable hands. "Behind him he leaves a shining wake."

I have spoken of sailing because we are on the same sea, moving in the same manner, facing the same joys and dangers, that men and women have experienced without change throughout time.

I can recall with crystal clarity one particular moment at sea.

We were headed north from South Carolina, where now I find my home, up to Connecticut, which was my home at the time. God launched a nor'easter, aimed directly on our path. Picture in your mind's eye those charming depictions of God's nostrils and mouth sending forth blasts that create storms. Charming, but only depicted after the storm. How it blew and blew for three days until, at last, it blew itself out. Proud creatures, we would venture forth each day, bringing all our might and courage, bending to the task. But it proved fruitless, and we surrendered and returned to our little redoubt to lick our wounds.

At last, we awoke, and the storm was gone. We smiled at one another, enthusiastic to head out after having to make peace with our paralysis. We can find our way again. Our arm is strong after all. God has taught us that he is in charge. Unlike Job, our chore was simply patience, not the suffering that the loss of God, Job's highest joy, occasioned. We had no evil detractors, mutineers in the supposed cause of God, blaming us for the storm.

As we entered the true seas of the God of offshore, at last free of impressive man-made intracoastal waterways, free to be in his majestic realms, we were treated to something rich and rare. The storms bearing down at his hand and at his command, whip up the seas ferociously. Making them impassable for all but the rash and imprudent, to be swallowed up and forgotten.

God had prepared a surprise, as he has done here with Job. Innocent, struck down, faithful through his own raging, confounded but his forever relational self, hanging on to the rudder of God's love for him until his hands are blue.

After this kind of hard three-day weather blow—multiply that by a factor without number for Job—we go out into the seas that he commands. Instead of wind and waves, or the messy residue of that, a marvel awaits that takes our breath away. The rollers are huge, evidence of the power of God Almighty simply being God Almighty. Majestic in the creation formed, maintained, and preserved at his hand.

The rollers are massive in scale, two to three stories high, of dimensions familiar to God, whose majestic habitat is not that of hawk, wild ox, raven, horse, ostrich, or even Behemoth and Leviathan. When we enter into these swells and descend, we cannot see the horizon but only the trough where our now tiny boat holds us. Walls of water on each side. A thing "too wonderful to know," as Job will confess shortly.

Here is the remarkable thing, the truly marvelous thing God has made and that he wills to show us. Majestic beauty, power, and transcendence come down to earth, at the bottom of the surface of the sea, where the world gives way to him and him alone. Where we see the creation as he sees it. The place that Job is struggling to find, and that God, who loves him, his most special friend in whom he has placed his faith and his own life, is taking him to.

The surface of the huge rollers, swallowing us and our most dwarfed craft, is as smooth as smooth can be. We are lifted high and we slide down the surface of the waves where all we see is water all around us, and the ride is sublime. "Behind him he leaves a shining wake."

Job has entered the rollers whose surface has not been smooth and whose scary depths of despair and anguish have caused all light to go out. Descending into the deepest trough, without God's sky for reassurance as he seeks to rise again and glimpse the heavens he once knew. God is speaking to him, and he is on his way to restoration.

Behind him he too will leave a shining wake.

Response and Restoration

Then Job answered the LORD:

"I know that thou canst do all things,
    and no purpose of thine can be thwarted.
'Who is this that hides counsel without knowledge?'
Therefore I have spoke of things I did not understand,
    things too wonderful for me, which I did not know.
'Hear, and I will speak;
    I will question you, and you declare to me.'
I had heard of thee by the hearing of the ear,
    but now my eye sees thee;
therefore I despise myself,
    and repent in dust and ashes." (Job 42:1–6)

Twice in this brief response, Job places the words God addressed to him in his discourse, on his own lips. God's speech forms part of Job's response. We have noted above that here we have a subtle resolution, Job and God, God and Job. Job has spoken of things beyond his ken, in the vortex of his suffering and his loss of the God formerly familiar to him. He has now seen things too wonderful for him to know and they urge upon him this response.

In order to know when and where the resolution of the book of Job comes, we need to remember what launched the journey before us. Job has seen God face to face. He has entered the plane where the familiar and the alien, the God whom he once knew and the God whom he did not want, have met and found resolution in a manner he did not know before. He has heard with the hearing of the ear, and he has lived in the company of God, who gives and who also takes away. Now his eye has seen him.

We might consider this a good place for the book to stop. Job has been transformed after his long and painful ordeal. God has lifted him into the realms of his majesty. Job recants of the two-dimensional account of God he has drawn upon, after having been visited with the transforming power of God himself. "Now my eye sees you."

In reality, however, this acknowledgment comes from the Job still on the ash-heap. At one level, one might conclude that this makes it even more profound. Is this the resolution of the book, however? Can Job not have his life back?

The crux of the book's movement and drama was revealed to us in the opening two chapters. Satan told God that no one would continue in relationship with him for no other reason than God's own self. Job's loyalty and faithfulness to God was only predicated, said Satan, on the blessings he had received at God's hand. God placed his absolute trust in Job and allowed him to be reduced to the barest minimum. And so, the book unfolds in accordance with this main governing reality.

Job has no idea of the wager. Only we do. The resolution that he finds comes without God ever revealing what the stakes were, behind or above the scene as it were. In his confession and acknowledgment that now he knows God as he truly is, in his majesty and authority, revealed to Job personally by God, one could say that Satan has lost.

But the book does not move from this dramatic acknowledgment to Job's full physical restoration directly. A book ending here might be spiritually profound. But Job is where he was when the horrible divestment began.

A very brief scene now unfolds. God addresses the three friends. Job is not within earshot. He renders a verdict over them. They have not spoken of God rightly, as has Job his servant. In whatever manner Job needed to be lifted onto another plane, and his account of God transformed, the friends were always wrong in what they said about God. Job has spoken of God rightly because he refused to accept the account of God being thrust at him. Instead, he sought the God of his former life, now inside the suffering and anguish which had become his lot.

We know Job does not hear this exchange, because the verdict falls in the context of instructions to the friends, that they are to make offerings on account of the wrath of God being visited upon them for their conduct and the content of their speaking with Job. Theirs is the wrath of God, and this is his own personal exchange with the three concerning their present fate before God. The God they have presumed to speak for in the context of Job's suffering.

This brief episode is compressed, and one must follow it closely. God doesn't say, "Ask Job to pray for you." To do that, Job would be brought into awareness of the circumstances and the details of the exchange. Instead, God simply says to Eliphaz, you and your comrades make the appropriate offerings I have given instruction to you about. "And Job will pray for you." A simple indicative statement. It is as though God knows this about Job, though he has had no exchange with him on the matter.

Who was Job before the ordeal he has now walked through? He was a man of prayer. During seasons of feasting, he arose every morning, offered sacrifices, and prayed for his sons. This is part and parcel of the description of Job with which the book opens. "In the land of Uz there lived a man whose name was Job. This man was blameless and upright; he feared God and shunned evil."

Can one be disinterestedly the friend and servant of God? "Blameless and upright; fearing God and shunning evil" while on the ash-heap? Can one pray for enemies as one has prayed for loved ones, sons now lost? Friends who made the lot he had to endure, double in severity. We only know one thing. Job prayed for the three, the word "friends" not being erased from the record.

We must presume that in this one quiet sentence, after all the drama preceding, Satan is now roundly defeated. Routed from the field of play, never to be seen again in Job's life with God. Job's trust and faith in God vindicated and triumphally. No fanfare, but the simple statement we have been waiting for, which constitutes the true resolution of the book. "And God restored the fortunes of Job when he had prayed for his friends."

The former and the latter Job, the same Job, transformed by his encounter with God. The same God, who gave and took away, and who Job discovered in the majesty of his creation. The world he alone knows, shared with Job, his friend. The man of prayer, "blameless and upright; fearing God and shunning evil," now on the higher plane of fellowship with God. His majesty and his condescension visited upon the Job in whom he has utmost pride. And now, redoubled pride.

Job Alive Again
The Book's Finale

After Job had prayed for his friends, the Lord restored his fortunes and gave him twice as much as he had before. All his brothers and sisters and everyone who had known him before came and ate with him in his house. They comforted and consoled him over all the trouble the Lord had brought on him, and each one gave him a piece of silver and a gold ring. The Lord blessed the latter part of Job's life more than the former part. He had fourteen thousand sheep, six thousand camels, a thousand yoke of oxen and a thousand donkeys. And he also had seven sons and three daughters. The first daughter he named Jemimah, the second Keziah and the third Keren-Happuch. Nowhere in all the land were there found women as beautiful as Job's daughters, and their father granted them an inheritance along with their brothers. After this, Job lived a hundred and forty years; he saw his children and their children to the fourth generation. And so Job died, an old man and full of years. (Job 42:10–17, NIV)

I have taught the book of Job many times. On occasion it has been remarked, or I have said myself, that after all Job has endured—the drama which constitutes the length and breadth of the present book—it would have been a great pleasure to have this final majestic restoration occupy more space than it does.

So let us go be with him in the space given to him at the end.

To be with Job in his joy and among the comforters who arrive to console him. To pull up a seat at his rich table and enjoy the feast with him. To bring him a precious gift. The man who prayed for his enemies and who, after having done that, found his fortunes restored. A resurrection into a latter life, twice as rich as what he had previously known. His exile into a far land over. The "Book Five" of his Psalter. His Songs of Ascent and Alleluia.

To have him show us his three daughters and to admire with him their beauty. To be treated to the rarity of their receipt of a grand inheritance.

It would be our fate to bid him adieu, the Job who would out-live us. He who would live far more years than the former Job, seeing four generations of children sit on his lap and feast at his table. Enjoying the inheritance left by him. Maybe even hearing the story we have been privileged to hear. Not from the book of Job, but from his own lips. As precious to them as God's words to Job from the whirlwind.

Things too wonderful to know.

Conclusion

The heavens are telling the glory of God;
    and the firmament proclaims his handiwork.
Day to day pours forth speech,
    and night to night declares knowledge.
There is no speech, nor are there words;
    their voice is not heard;
yet their voice goes out through all the earth,
    and their words to the end of the world.

In them he has set a tent for the sun,
which comes forth like a bridegroom leaving his chamber,
    and like a strong man runs its course with joy.
Its rising is from the end of the heavens,
    and its circuit to the end of them;
there is nothing hid from its heat. (Ps 19:1–6)

The purpose of this book has been to examine closely the place and function of the psalms of creation in the larger movement of the Psalter. To gain a better sense of their range and purpose, what distinguishes them, and what they share in the inspired world of the psalmist's expression. More particularly, to learn to appreciate how they come alongside the covenants that speak of God's personal relationship with the people of his electing love and purposes.

What we have come to see is how foundational praise of God in the majesty of creation is in the purposes of God. At those moments when Israel is facing hardship, exile, and apparent abandonment, these are the psalms that serve to remind Israel of the authority of God over all he has made and the promise inherent in that. He has authority over darkness and flood when these arise as realities in the life of his people.

We then turned to the particular case of Job. Our concern has been to understand the divine speeches, how they function, what they say, and why this is the terrain—as also in the Psalms—on which God decides to speak to Job and to resolve the harsh dilemma rising up inside of him. And just how they do that.

We have taken Job at his word in the response to what God says to him. In turn, we have sought to know how it is that what God has said has achieved this outcome and brought peace to his soul. Grand restoration and long life are given to him after he has heard what God has said and indicated its transforming power, and after he prayed for his friends. In this way Satan is defeated, cleared from the field of play, God's trust in Job is fully vindicated, and the former Job's life proves but a foretaste of the grandeur of the latter Job's.

God created the world. But that isn't something back in time only. He is continually creating, preserving, holding in order and stability every single thing he has made. He sits enthroned over the flood as I type this. As the General Thanksgiving puts it, "We bless you for our creation, preservation, and all the blessings of this life . . . for us and for all whom you have made." God creating and preserving is the ultimate act of prevenience. The bulwark against all foes. When we fear when the waters rise, he says, "Be still and know that I am God."

The early church fathers, in arguing with those who would diminish the identity of the Son vis-à-vis the Father, saw in the scriptures of Israel an assemblage of texts to which they had recourse. The Hebrew word for "beginning" or "first" was taken by them in key texts (Gen 1, Prov 8:22) together with the dual impress one can see in John 1, in a sense temporal but also implying agency. The Hebrew substantive *reshith* is the first word in Scripture and with the preposition *be*, we render "In the beginning" or "In beginning." In *reshith*. The potential lies in the same *bereshith* "in beginning," or "the agent of beginning."

Speaking of wisdom, in Proverbs 8, the author says, "The LORD brought me forth/begat/possessed me [as] the *reshith* of his ways." Athanasius and a host of interpreters saw here agency, as did their opponents. The debate was whether this agent was begotten or made. The Hebrew verb they held (in translation into Greek or for those who could make their way with Hebrew in the form they could get to it) was "to beget"—that is, generated from within the LORD himself. So, when John 1 says, "In the beginning was the Word, and the Word was with God, and the Word was God, the same was in the beginning with God," he is speaking of agency and temporality as indistinguishable.

For the purpose of our work here, what can be said, following from this logic? Practically everything that we have been saying, now with the deeper significance proper to it. The majesty of creation is that which has come into being through the Word of God. He is the active agency through whom all things were made. Creation is upheld by the two hands of the Father who made it and the Son through whom it was made.

John will continue, "In him was life, and the life was the light of men. The light shines in the darkness, and the darkness has not overcome it" (John 1:4).

In the psalms of creation, in the word spoken to Job, at the heart of these texts, there is the Life and the Life was the Light of men. He is the Light. Under signs and figures in the Psalms and in Job, and in the incarnation about which John speaks. "And the Word, the beginning, became flesh and we beheld His glory, the glory as of the only begotten of the Father, full of grace and truth."

The Voice going out into all the world—it is his voice. His voice over the waters, the same voice who prayed for his enemies, the voice who commands the winds and waves of our lives. The Voice alive and stilling the storms of all who call on him, as did, once upon a time, the people of Israel and most especially his singular servant, Job.

FOR FURTHER STUDY

The shift from form-critical emphasis on individual psalms, toward an appreciation of the Psalter as a collection, is often associated with B. S. Childs and his student Gerald H. Wilson, *The Editing of the Hebrew Psalter* (Chico, Calif.: Scholars Press, 1985). I depart from him over the interpretation of Books 4 and 5 and the presentation of the Davidic promise as this unfolds there (see "Royal Promises in the Canonical Books of Isaiah and the Psalms," in Christopher R. Seitz, *Word without End: The Old Testament as Abiding Theological Witness* [Waco, Tex.: Baylor University Press, 2004], 150–67). Nevertheless, his is the standard introduction to the main issues at stake in reading the Psalter as an editorially arranged whole.

Two of my former students follow a similar point of orientation: Brian T. German, *Psalms of the Faithful: Luther's Early Reading of the Psalter in Canonical Context* (Bellingham, Wash.: Lexham Press, 2017) and Andrew Witt, *A Voice without End: The Role of David in Psalms 3–14* (Winona Lake, Ind.: Eisenbrauns, 2021).

Recent works that challenge the idea of "wisdom literature" are Katharine Dell, *The Solomonic Corpus of "Wisdom" and Its Influence* (Oxford: Oxford University Press, 2020); Will Kynes, *An Obituary for "Wisdom Literature": The Birth, Death, and Intertextual Reintegration of a Biblical Corpus* (Oxford: Oxford University Press, 2019); Stuart Weeks, *An Introduction to the Study of Wisdom Literature* (London: T&T Clark, 2010). The Solomonic books have been reinstated as a grouping, leaving the book of Job free to be treated as its own special witness.

I have benefited from the brilliant treatment of Job by Karl Barth, found in *Church Dogmatics* IV.3.1, 383–461.

I have my own article-length contribution to the interpretation of the book of Job as a carefully arranged presentation in Christopher R. Seitz, "Job: Full-Structure, Movement, and Interpretation," *Interpretation* 43, no. 1 (1989): 5–17.

The poet and the songwriter referred to in "Book Four of the Psalter" are John O'Donohue, *To Bless the Space Between Us: A Book of Blessings* (New York: Doubleday, 2008), and Cory Asbury, "Faithful Wounds," in his album *To Love a Fool* (2020).